Under the Bl ____y

JIMMY GRAY

WITH MICHAEL O'GRADY

www.**HERO**BOOKS.digital

HEROBOOKS

PUBLISHED BY HERO BOOKS
1 WOODVILLE GREEN
LUCAN
CO. DUBLIN
IRELAND

Hero Books is an imprint of Umbrella Publishing
First Published 2022
Copyright © Jimmy Gray and Michael O'Grady 2022
All rights reserved

ISBN 9781910827512

Cover design and formatting: jessica@viitaladesign.com
Photographs: Sportsfile and the Gray family collection

Dedication

To Gretta

Contents

« ACKNOWLEDGEMENTS »

TO MY BELOVED and long-suffering wife Gretta, whose own achievements with the camogie board and Na Fianna are a matter of great pride to us, and without whose support and love I could not have done what I did within the GAA.

To my children John, Tom, Carmel and Annmarie – thank you. I am so proud of you and am so delighted that our love of sport was handed down to you. To my daughters-in-law Ann, Orla and Alison, who have enriched all of our lives and who have willingly embraced our Na Fianna life.

To my grandchildren Seán, Dónal, Laura, Dara and Aisling. I am so happy to see you grow and develop. I take pride in your successes as you journey through the stages of your lives.

To my sister Ita and brother Frank, my thanks for your love and support always.

To all who have supported me in the great community that is the GAA – in my spiritual home of Na Fianna, in Dublin and in Leinster… I thank you all for all you have done for me. I am delighted to see the progress of Dublin and of Na Fianna.

I got involved with the Dublin County Board in the early-70s, and it was obvious to us that change needed to take place if we were to survive. Even though he was slow to accept the fact, the late Jim King played a massive part in facilitating change in Dublin GAA. He was ably assisted by the late Mick Leahy and Donal Hickey. Both men did wonderful work during the early days. Paula

Lee was secretary and she ran a very efficient office. I really valued their support and enthusiasm.

Dublin GAA continues to prosper and grow, and while many people make that possible, John Costello as CEO, deserves great credit due to his leadership and commitment.

I had three years as chairman of Leinster GAA and I was a trustee for two periods of three years each. This period of my life opened my eyes to the amazing influence the GAA has on all aspects of life in every parish in the country. Every club plays its part in making the GAA such an impressive organisation and it fills my heart with pride.

The late Jim Boggan was a great friend of mine, and he left us much too early. He made a massive contribution to Crumlin GAA and to Dublin hurling. He was a humble man and he worked tirelessly in his efforts to promote the game. He helped out many a young person and kept them on the straight and narrow.

Thanks to Michael O'Grady, without whose persuasion this book would never have happened. As well as coaching teams he was a founder member of Friends of Dublin Hurling and it has played a big part in the promotion of hurling at all levels in Dublin.

To Liam Hayes and his team at Hero Books for all their assistance in making this production possible. Many thanks.

Jimmy Gray
March 2022

◄ ◄ ◆ ▷ ►

« CHAPTER 1 »

Beginnings

I WAS BORN on Berkeley Road in north Dublin, near the Mater Hospital. My father bought a house on Dargle Road in Drumcondra and we all lived there until we got married. My parents lived there for the rest of their lives.

My dad fought in the War of Independence to begin with, when he was with Seán McKeon in county Longford. During the Civil War, he was interned in Dungiven in county Derry. He never really spoke with me or anyone about those years.

Both my parents were from Longford. Dad was from Moyne in north Longford where the family had the local post office. My mother hailed from Ardagh, in south Longford, but they met in Dublin. My mother moved to the city and worked in a shop on Capel Street, while dad worked for a fruit merchant. That's how they met.

During the Civil War my dad's family was broken up, like so many families during that tragic period in our history.

My dad had three brothers, Michael, James and Denis. Denis went to America, and Michael and James were also part of Seán McKeon's outfit. Seán McKeon was known as the 'Blacksmith of Ballinalee' and he was the boss of the local IRA during the War of Independence.

When the truce came, my father was opposed to it, whereas Michael and James were in support of it. They fell out, and sadly I believe they didn't speak until 1936, when their mother died. Our house on Dargle Road in Drumcondra became a hub for lots of callers, lots of visitors from Longford and other parts, and they were always very welcome. Cards were played every Sunday night, the most popular being games of 25, 15 and 110. Lots of meetings were held in our house as well.

My father was involved in Fianna Fáil, and they would have their meetings under our roof sometimes too. Na Fianna also held meetings in our house, especially in the early days. My mother and father were very involved in the club, my mother especially. She ran sales of work and many other kinds of fundraisers for the club.

We loved all the callers because they always brought something with them. It was a great house for comings and goings, and nobody objected to it. My mother loved it, even though it meant a lot of work for her.

ON THE ROAD, we learned our football.

There was no hurling in my life at that stage. My brother Dinny was an expert at making rag balls and that's how we played. The balls wouldn't last too long when they got wet. The guards were always moving us on and, once, we got a summons for playing on the road. My mother, God be good to her, went to the court and said to the judge, 'Where else can they play… there's no park nearby!'

I had two wonderful parents. They made sacrifices for me and it was only when they were gone that I came to appreciate it.

Every Christmas, Easter and summer we went to my mother's home place in Longford. There was a lovely lake there, and we could swim and fish to our hearts content. I have some wonderful memories of those times. The lake would overflow in wintertime and the Board of Works had to drain it.

It was a fine big lake, three miles long and one mile wide, and my mother used to say with a smile on her face, 'Oh, my brother has a big farm of one hundred acres – most of it covered in water!' I worked on the farm with my uncle during the summer holidays and I got a wonderful introduction to farm life and I enjoyed it immensely. I have a lot of great friends down there still.

I have two brothers and two sisters. I was the eldest. Dinny came next. Then came my sisters Marie and Ita. Frank was the youngest of the family. Dinny and Marie have gone to their eternal reward. Frank is alive and well, and very involved with Na Fianna. We went to school in St Patrick's Drumcondra. Dublin was very soccer-orientated at the time so there wasn't much gaelic games in the schools. Frankie Byrne, who played for Meath, was one of our teachers. Paddy Henry from Sligo was also there. He won an All-Ireland medal with Dublin in 1942.

There were a lot of pupils in the school but nobody took an interest in promoting gaelic games. We put pressure on Paddy Henry 'to take' a school team, and he did for a while. We weren't much good as most of our players were soccer players and had no interest in gaelic football. We took part in Cumann na mBunscol inter-school competitions, but we got big beatings when we met schools like Marino.

Most of those school games took place in the Fifteen Acres in the Phoenix Park. It was very awkward for us to get there... we had to get two buses, and then we had a good walk from Islandbridge up to the pitches. A good mile at least! For some reason, Paddy Henry stopped looking after us and so we had to manage ourselves... Charlie McCauley and Shay Gibbons took command. We played Denmark Street in the Fifteen Acres one afternoon and, after the game, we were walking down to the bus-stop at Islandbridge and we started slagging each other. A few punches were thrown, but we were well able to look after ourselves.

MY FIRST REAL contact with gaelic games were our weekly trips to Croke Park, which was just a short walk away from our home. Both my father and my mother were very interested in hurling and football. My dad played junior football for Cavan, but he must have been illegal of course... he was from Longford!

We went to club matches on Sunday mornings at 11.30am, and sometimes we went back for county games in the afternoon. Chicky Curran was the groundsman.

If Chicky was there, we got in for free. If not, we hoped that somebody would lift us over the stile.

After doing the Primary Cert, I went to Coláiste Mhuire in Parnell Square. It was an all-Irish school run by the Christian Brothers. It was a great school and the Brothers were very interested in gaelic games.

Thursday was sports day, when we would go to the school grounds on the banks of the Liffey at Islandbridge. We didn't have a lot of success, though we qualified for an under-16 final against Westland Row CBS in Croke Park. They were one of the top teams at the time. They beat us, but it was wonderful to get to play in Croke Park. It was in Coláiste Mhuire that I was introduced to hurling. There were some fantastic Brothers there… Br Ó Cearnaigh, and Br Ó Faoláin and Br Ó Catháin… just to mention a few. After doing the Inter Cert, I was sent to a school in Wales. It's a long story, but I will tell it as best as I can. My mother always had it in her mind to make a priest out of me. I had an uncle who was a priest in Newport in south Wales. It was arranged that I would go to a Carmelite School in Aberystwyth in Wales.

I regarded it as an adventure, but all the rest of my family didn't share my enthusiasm. On the morning I was leaving home to go to Dun Laoghaire to start my journey, Dinny, my younger brother, was bawling his eyes out in the kitchen.

My dad came with me as far as Dun Laoghaire, and I got the boat – The Hibernia – to Holyhead. I had my instructions on how to get to my destination, once I reached Holyhead. I got the train to Crewe, changed at Shrewsbury… and I met my uncle at Aberystwyth.

He drove me up to the school. It was about 10 o'clock at night when we got there. I was brought straight to the dormitory with nothing to eat.

The school was a boarding school with only about twenty boarders. There was only one other Irish lad… John O'Hehir. The two of us would sometimes watch the boat heading for Rosslare and that added to our homesickness. I was there for 12 months and did a certificate exam at the end of the school year.

We were then transferred to Llandeilo further south in Wales. We had nicer accommodation in this school… two people to each room. We started playing rugby there too, and I really enjoyed it. We had some very good players.

We wound up in the South Wales Colleges semi-final. Only about three of us had played rugby before, but we became fairly good at it. Llanelli were the top rugby school team at the time. We played them and they beat us by three points in a great game. I played in the centre.

We had two lads from Poland on each wing and, when they took off, you wouldn't catch them. So we would work the ball out to them… and off they would go. They were unstoppable. They were two fascinating lads. One of their mothers paid a visit during our time there and told us that during the war they walked from Poland to Germany to avoid the Russians.

I sat the final exam – the equivalent of the Leaving Cert and, thankfully, I passed it. When I got back to Dublin, I really didn't know what to do. I was getting hints about going to a seminary. But I made up my mind that I wasn't going to go down that road.

My father quizzed me about what my plans were.

'Ah I'll get a job somewhere,' I told him.

He reminded me that there were very few jobs going at the time. He came home one day and gave me a bit of paper and said, 'Go down and talk to that man!'

The man's name was Jimmy McCourt. He worked for Connolly Shaw – a fruit merchant and a shipping company. I was interviewed by Jimmy and, much to my delight, I got the job. My pay was 30 shillings a week… good money at the time.

I wound up in charge of shipping in Connolly Shaw. I enjoyed the shipping part of it as there was great variety and you would meet lots of different people. There were a lot of trade restrictions during those times and lots of forms had to be completed for each transaction. In the newspaper, one day, there was an advert for a trade advisor for Córas Tráchtála, the Irish Export Board, and I just wrote to it more out of curiosity than anything else. I was called for an interview, and got the job. My title was 'Trade Advisor Shipping'. So that started me on a whole new career as it were. My first assignment was to London and then to Liverpool, where I was manager. I was terrified of Liverpool because of its reputation, but I liked every minute of it. The Scousers were wonderful people.

I TRAVELLED ALL over England, Wales and Scotland.

Mike Killeen was the boss in Córas Tráchtála. The Sugar Company was looking for a good shipping adviser as they were going into the export market. This was all new to them as up to then all they did was produce sugar. General Costello, the CEO, was a tough man but a great leader, and I always got on well with him. He suggested that they look for somebody from Coras Tráchtála.

Anyway, the General got on to Mike Killeen and said, 'Can we have Jimmy for a year?' So I went to the Sugar Company. At the end of the year I got a letter from Córas Tráchtála reminding me that the year was up… I was due back to them.

I didn't really want to go back, so I got on to my boss and he went to the General, who spoke to Mike Killeen and, as a result of their chat, I stayed with the Sugar Company. So that's how I ended up there. It was a great place to work. I spent many happy years there.

Chris Comerford became CEO of the Sugar Company and he was a wonderful man, and a great worker. He saved the company with his hard work and good business-like decisions. He hails from Windgap in Kilkenny and he loves hurling… and we are great friends to this day.

I MET GRETTA at a CJ Kickhams club dance in St Peter's Hall, in Phibsborough. My sister, a cousin and a friend of hers were at the dance. My cousin introduced me to her friend… Gretta O'Shea from Bannow, Co Wexford. We went out for about two and a half years.

Then Gretta went off to America. We kept in touch. She came home for a holiday in 1958 and we got back together again. When she returned to America again, we agreed she would come home for good the next time.

We got married in 1959, in St Agatha's Catholic Church on North William Street. We were touring Ireland on our honeymoon and were on our way to Killarney, when I received a call from Jimmy Nolan, a Dublin team selector, telling me we had a game in Kilkenny on the Sunday and… I was to be there. When I told him I was on my honeymoon and heading to Kerry, he said, 'Sure that's only over the road from Kilkenny. I'll see you on Sunday!' With Gretta's blessing, we travelled to Kilkenny, and I played the game and we stayed overnight. I got some abuse from my mother and my mother-in-law when we got home.

WE USED TO go down to Bannow fairly often.

Bannow is a gorgeous area, and we loved the beach. Gretta's dad was a builder, and he built the local school as well as some houses. Theirs was a fairly large family, but most of them went to America. Gretta has one sister and one brother living here in Ireland.

We bought a house in Grove Park, between Finglas and Ballymun. It wasn't our best investment so we sold it and moved to Willow Park Drive, where we now are and it is a lovely spot.

Gretta is a great lady and, I must admit, it took me a long time to appreciate it. I was away a lot, either on business or on GAA affairs. She put up with me all the time. We have four of the best children that one would ever wish to have.

Gretta actually reared the family.

I tell her she will go straight to heaven, but she doesn't believe me.

◄ ◄ ◆ ▷ ►

GRETTA GRAY

I met Jim in St Peter's Hall, in Phibsborough, in 1953 at a dance organised by the Rainbow Social Club, the brainchild of some members of CJ Kickhams GAA club. The ban on foreign dances was in existence but these bright lads got around it by organising it in the club. Jim and I got on well together and dated, but then I had America in mind and emigrated there in October 1955. Letters went back and forth between us... when I came home in 1958, for my uncle's wedding, Jim proposed.

I said, 'Yes' but, as I had commitments in America, I had to return to New York.

Jim's late sister Marie had a friend who was an air hostess with Aer Lingus and she brought my engagement ring to me in New York. It fitted perfectly... how romantic was that? I came home in May 1959, and we got married in September that year. I had a wish to honeymoon in Jersey, but Jim said we should just hire a car and tour Ireland. I didn't realise that touring Ireland included a stop in Kilkenny for Jim to play in a Walsh Cup hurling match!

◄ ◄ ◆ ▷ ►

IN DUE TIME the kids came along... John, Tom, Carmel and Annmarie. We were saddened at the loss of our third child, Dominic in 1964, the day after his birth.

John was a good hurler, but didn't take it seriously. Tom was a good footballer and is still very much involved managing teams at all levels. The two girls took up camogie and really enjoyed it. Both of them played for Dublin, as well as Na Fianna.

The main reason they took to camogie was that Gretta was now one of the main organisers of camogie in the club, compliments of Seán Clerkin. Annmarie was playing at the age of six and, one day, had to be lifted off the pitch because she was so cold.

Three of the family are accountants, and Carmel is principal of Scoil Chaitríona. Carmel was a great student and when she was doing her Masters in UCD she was encouraged to apply for a lecturing job. But she wasn't interested. She always wanted to be a teacher.

I am so proud of my family and what they have achieved in life; first and foremost in character, then in sport, and above all, in their concern for others.

◄ ◁ ◆ ▷ ►

JOHN GRAY

Na Fianna is dad's life, and he loves winning. We were playing Dalkey Mitchels in Ringsend in a Minor Championship game. Dad was in charge of the team, and Tom and myself would go to all the games with him. Anyway, we only had 15 players and, as luck would have it, we lost two players during the first-half. The referee came to dad at the start of the second-half and told him he would need 15 players for the restart.

Dad put myself and Tom on to play in the full-forward line. The only problem was… we were only six or seven years of age. Anyway, we stood there and did the best we could. Halfway during the second-half, the ref told my dad he could take us off. But when he came in to take us off, we said we didn't want to go off. We were just delighted to be playing minor hurling years before our time. All I know is we won the game easily. We had some very good players.

He often chided me for giving up hurling. It is to my eternal regret, that I didn't stick with it.

My son Seán was a very skilful hurler. Seán played in goal and he made some top-class saves in the Dublin Féile final. We qualified to represent Dublin in the National Féile finals and we played our games on the Ballyhale Shamrocks' pitch. Dad was there shouting and urging the boys on. He is extremely competitive, but when the game was over, he was very complimentary of the effort made by all the players and mentors.

Dad is multi-talented. He is a skilled carpenter. He built all of the wardrobes, kitchen cabinets and living room wall units in our home. We spent a couple of holidays cabin cruising on the Shannon. He told us he intended building his own cabin cruiser, eventually. It never happened, mainly because he was so busy at work and attending to GAA affairs.

TOM GRAY

I played a little bit of hurling at under-14 and under-16 level, but football became my game. Dad had a natural preference for hurling but he was very happy to see me playing football. He never pressurised us to play a particular game… he was just happy that we were into hurling, football and camogie. He was very busy with GAA matters so he wasn't a regular on the sideline at our games. My uncle Dinny looked after my age group at under-13 football and we were reasonably competitive. Later on, at under-15 and under-16, we had other mentors but our performances deteriorated to the extent that we were bottom of the league in under-16. I always remember dad coming out to one of our games and observing that we had plenty of potential.

The following year he took on coaching the team at minor level, despite being county chairman. The following two seasons, we reached two county finals in succession and were runners-up in the leagues. St Vincent's had an excellent team in that age group and they were too good for us. That was a lifelong learning for me in both business and sport, as it demonstrated what improvements could be achieved if a team is properly organised with a clear gameplan and with the coaching to execute the plan.

After my last year at minor level, he took on the minor hurling team which then proceeded to win the championship, again demonstrating his coaching and management ability. Obviously, he had a close relationship with Heffo at the time and you could see that influence in many ways in how he managed us. I sometimes heard Heffo and himself discussing football issues and, looking back now, I must say they were ahead of their time.

Dad was chairman of the Dublin County Board for nine years in the 70s, which was a time of great change in Dublin with a growing population and new clubs coming on board... and the difficulty of getting suitable land for playing pitches and clubhouses.

It coincided with the upsurge of interest in gaelic football because of the successful county team. When he retired as county chairman, he went to a series of retirement dinners. He had a speech which the family could nearly recite word-for-word, the core of which was the importance of community in a big capital city.

He saw Dublin GAA as much more than providing football and hurling games for the masses. He believed in the importance of the community element in a successful club, and that a successful club/county gave people a sense of identity and pride. He believed this first and foremost in the context of a GAA club in its own community but he also saw the success of the county teams in a wider sense for Dublin people who perhaps weren't directly involved in the GAA... and the pride they felt in a successful county team. I didn't appreciate that as a youngster, but as I got older, I began to see the importance of the community element of the club and county. My own club Na Fianna, is a very good example of what I am talking about.

He is now in his nineties, and I am amazed at his interest and enthusiasm for Dublin hurling and football. I visited him recently and we watched the Dublin vs

Galway football league game in Salthill. He was commenting on various good and bad moves, and he almost went into the television when Dublin conceded a rather soft goal. He never misses a game of hurling or football and he loves being around the club watching the busyness of the place.

I have been managing the Dublin under-20 team for the past few years and I always get a 'quality control call' after a game to let me know what I did well and not so well. He has an aversion to short passing in both football and hurling which he has communicated wide and far!! And he was never afraid to tell me that I was the problem, if the teams I managed engaged in that practice. However, what I found interesting was that when you teased the point out with him, his true aversion is to short passing with no pace and no purpose, and who can disagree with that. I have learned so much from him, and it has made me a better manager. He is excellent at finding the right position for players and where best to put them to improve the team.

CARMEL GRAY

I have a few stories that show aspects of dad's character.

The first one shows his loyalty and commitment to his word. He had been playing football and hurling with Dublin. In 1957, a gang of them decided to opt for hurling and drop the football at inter-county level.

Some of the players eventually went back to the football and won an All-Ireland medal in 1958. Dad stuck to his word, however, and stayed with the hurlers and thereby lost out on an All-Ireland medal. It's a matter of great disappointment to him that he never won an All-Ireland, but he gave a commitment and he stuck to his word.

It was never about his ego. Anything he did was never to promote himself, but because it was the right thing to do.

We grew up with two persons really. One was our dad... and the other was Jimmy Gray.

He was in Croke Park one day with my six-year-old nephew Seán and, for some reason, Seán got separated from Jimmy. Seán knew that all he had to do was go up to one of the stewards and say, 'Where is Jimmy Gray?' Wherever he goes, he is well known. Everywhere we went, he would end up talking to people that we had never seen before. We got used to that.

In relation to camogie, he always encouraged us but he spent most of his time with the boys. My mum was our main support. I remember we were in a very important camogie final and dad couldn't come to the game because he was training the minor footballers. We were devastated that he couldn't make it. He was committed to the minor footballers, so they came first. But my mam was always there and we appreciated that. He was very proud of our achievements. His mantra was that you needed skill, brains and strength to be a good player.

Kevin Heffernan was a great friend of his and he was devastated when he couldn't go to Kevin's funeral. as he was unwell at the time himself.

We grew up with two parents very committed to volunteerism. Dad could be doing anything in the club... like cutting the grass, pulling a pint... training teams, anything! He was on numerous committees down through the years. As he gets older he still is very committed to the club and wants to know who is in charge of the various teams, and how they are doing. He is as interested in an under-11 team as he is in the senior team.

I'd say he would be hard pushed to know what I did in college, but he knew I did okay. He always told us that he didn't mind what we decided to do as long as we were happy. I did a Masters after I started teaching. At the graduation my father was speaking to Professor Joe Carty and he said to him, something like, 'Could Carmel become a lecturer in UCD?'

Joe being very polite said, 'Oh yes, of course!'

So, that became... 'Joe Carty told me you should be a lecturer!'

We learned early on that our parents were committed to other projects and, therefore, we shared them with other people and groups. My mum was chairperson of the Dublin Camogie Board, as well as very involved in Na Fianna. My mum was also the boss in the house. Very occasionally dad would get stubborn, but that was rare. He rebuilt the living room in 1975 and it has never been touched since. Communication between my parents was marvellous. One time, my mam was going away on holidays and she said to us, 'I just hope your father doesn't do anything while I'm away!'

He did the kitchen floor, of course, which mam didn't really want.

Twice, we went boating on the Shannon. He would bring a large supply of Erin's Food steamed puddings and he took great pleasure in doing the cooking. He loved those holidays. We were playing a camogie championship semi-final game in Silverpark in Kilmacud one evening. There was a referee who did not like our style of play. We had one excellent player who if she only looked at the ball there would be a free against her. Anyway, dad wasn't impressed by the referee's performance and he left her know his feelings.

My mum was chairperson of the Dublin board at the time, so the referee stopped the game and dad was ordered to leave the pitch. So, reluctantly, he walked down to the corner flag and stopped. He was told he had to walk to the end of the next pitch as well. He was furious. As he approached the dressing-rooms, he met a fan who enquired why he wasn't watching the game. He told him the story and finished by saying, 'If that ref was a man, I would have hit him'.

My first memories are of going to matches was to watch my mum play in goal in the Phoenix Park. I was less than seven then. We used to go to Croke Park and I brought a book as I was too bored and too little.

My father was very involved, so we would spend most of our Sundays at matches somewhere watching him or my mother play. We went to a lot of the Dublin football games in the 1970s when the team was doing really well. They used to come up to Na Fianna on big game days. There were no fancy hotels in those days… they would come for scrambled eggs and toast.

I can remember running around the field getting the players autographs… and I still have them somewhere. Dad is my GAA hero. He has been involved at every level in the GAA. I have seen my mum and dad putting a massive amount of time in voluntarily, and probably being out of pocket as well. In that sense, for me, they symbolise 'the hero' in the GAA.

ANNMARIE GRAY

My delivery room might as well have been the Na Fianna clubhouse, as I was born into the GAA and it became an integral part of our lives. Both mam and dad were hugely involved in the club and in the Dublin GAA and camogie scene. Everything was dictated by the GAA season and the needs of Dublin GAA and the Na Fianna club… from when we could take our holidays to our extra-curricular activities.

A lot of my childhood memories are of being in the club… training, playing hide and seek, making sandwiches, sales of works, Feile na Fianna fairs, helping at bingo, stapling raffle tickets together, even part of photoshoots for a huge picture that graced the entrance to the club for many years. In the very early days, there were also executive meetings in our house.

In the 70s, of course, it was travelling up and down the country to Dublin matches, listening to Johnny Cash and The Dubliners, and belting out Seven Drunken Nights. *Being the last one to leave Croke Park after matches, Carmel and I would run or cartwheel across the pitch to meet him and Kevin Heffernan when we finally saw them coming out. Kevin used to call me blondie or fairy every time he'd see me. The Heffo days are when I honed my receptionist skills, especially around All-Irelands and the ticket frenzy. We would be tasked to answer the phone and find out who was calling and why, and pass on the message to Dad. He would be annoyed if we forgot.*

We would meet so many people. I used to enjoy watching him talking to somebody and, afterwards, we would say to him, 'Who was that?' And he would say, 'I have no idea!' He loved talking to people... even total strangers. He would always find a point of connection – Where are you from? What's your local GAA club? What soccer team do you support? Do you play golf? More recently, when he was in hospital, he kept the doctors and nurses from their work asking the same questions and telling them all about their local GAA club and the people he knew from there.

There was never any doubt that we would play the games. Carmel and I were on the first ever juvenile under-11 team, and played even though I was only six years old! Our first-ever game played to a 0-0 draw in freezing conditions, and I was carried off the pitch frozen at the final whistle. I don't think I even touched the ball once.

Dad was so caught up with Dublin GAA - and his job which took him away a lot to Liverpool or down the country - that he didn't have much opportunity to be involved in our playing of the game or to be able to come to our matches when we were young. In fact, in those days, parents didn't tend to come to your matches often. Though when we were playing senior club and county camogie for Dublin he would come to some of our matches, and you would see him on the sideline or hear him as he would get quite vocal being supportive and offering 'helpful' advice to the referee. He would get quite excited watching a game no matter if it was a senior county game or an under-11 friendly match.

One time we went to see my nephew, Dara, playing a Féile final. I recall having to hold on to him and say, 'Da, they are only 14... take it easy!' He was getting so worked up. Even at games now he will be heard shouting, 'Will you put your two hands on the hurley'... and 'For God's sake, stop that short-passing... it drives me mad!'

He was very supportive after a game – we might have lost by 10 goals, but he would point out that we had five missed chances and five of the other team's goals were flukes – so actually, it was a very close game!

I love hurling and certainly get that from him. When I played senior, it dominated my time and I gave up going out or on holidays so as not to miss matches or training. I played until I was 40.

I never saw dad play hurling or football. I work in the Irish Film Institute and when I got my first tour of the film archives, I was delighted to learn that they had films of all the All-Ireland finals. I arranged to have the 1961 All-Ireland final transferred to video and I gave it to dad for Christmas. We all sat down and watched it after our Christmas dinner. He was so disappointed that it didn't show the controversial point that Tipp got. Though we enjoyed slagging him for soloing out of the back line.

It was great to finally get a sense of the match that we had heard so much about growing up. When we launched our GAA All-Ireland series on DVD, he pulled out his address book and phoned many of the greats to ask them to come along for the launch, making it a success. In fact, working at the IFI, I discovered dad's film career – participating in Rooney *with John Gregson. Filmed in 1957 it is a story of a Dublin binman who gets picked to play for Dublin in the All-Ireland final the week before the match (though they are wearing Kilkenny colours). Dad was in one of the games , though being in goal he was too far way to pick out. It was great to hear his stories of the film and of John Gregson. We were also at a screening of* Rocky Road to Dublin, *the seminal Peter Lennon film from 1967. There is a scene of a hurling match in Croke Park and at one stage you see a man running onto the pitch to help an injured player. Dad turned to me and said, 'I think that's me,' and indeed it was!*

The first time I became aware that he was 'famous' was when I saw him interviewed on television. Wavin were promoting their new unbreakable hurley, and Dad was giving his opinion of the hurley and hitting a few balls.

He definitely loves both football and hurling but there is no doubt that hurling is his No 1. I asked him once, how many Sam Maguires would he give back for one Liam MacCarthy… and his answer was, 'Every f***ing one of them!'

When dad was looking after the Dublin hurlers there was headline in the Evening Press… Gray is Optimistic. *That made me laugh out loud – because of course he is, he is the most positive person in the world. He always emphasised to us the importance of health and happiness, and it has been my motto for life.*

Jimmy Gray with his father Tommy and a younger sibling in the 30s and (inset) with his brothers Frank and Dinny. Taking centre-stage (below) with his extended family during his playing days with Dublin in the 60s.

« CHAPTER 2 »

My Club

NA FIANNA, LIKE a lot of institutions in this country, was born out of a dispute with the CJ Kickhams club, a very old club in Dublin with adult members only.

They won All-Irelands in hurling and football in the late 1890s and early 1900s. They were mainly comprised of members of the drapery trade.

The older members in the club were very conservative, at least that is what we felt.

Seán O'Neill, Bobby Kane and Harry Giltrapp, and other younger members started underage hurling and football and were quite successful. As a consequence, there was a very large number of younger members in the club. It came to a head at an AGM, when there was a dispute about who was entitled to vote.

The older members of the club walked out of the meeting and that precipitated a very bitter six-month dispute. It was covered in the papers and brought up at the Drapers' Union. It was actually very nasty at times. Numerous committees were set up to sort it out. Paddy McNamee from Antrim, a former GAA president, chaired one particular meeting.

The story goes that Pádraig Ó Caoimh, the secretary in Croke Park, said to Tom Fitzpatrick, our leader, 'This is going to drag on and on, so why don't ye start your own club?'

WE HELD A meeting and Tom Fitzpatrick, a brilliant man and the first chairman of the club, stated that Pádraig Ó Caoimh had a point and it needed to be given serious consideration. So the outcome was that the meeting decided that we should start our own club. Another meeting was called to set up the new club and officers were elected.

Several names were proposed for our new club name.

One was Glasnevin Gaels.

Cathal Ó Feinneadha proposed that we name the new club Na Fianna.

His reason was that this name couldn't be anglicised. We then moved on to picking our club colours.

Again, we had lots of suggestions.

We considered the colours of the local school, St Vincent's, which was a boarding school as well as a day school. Their colours were yellow and blue. Another proposal was that we should go for all white, and the logic there was that a lot of our players were small and they would look bigger in all white jerseys and, believe it or not, this was adopted.

However, these colours didn't last for long.

We played St Vincent's on a very wet night in Croke Park. As there was going to be a clash of colours we, being the younger club, had to change. Tom Fitzpatrick, our chairman, had a friend in the ESB, who was involved with a junior club in Inchicore called St Michael's.

They only lasted a year or two.

So we borrowed their colours... yellow and blue.

We lost the game by a point. When Tom was about to return the jerseys, he was told that St Michael's were no longer competing. So, we got our first set of jerseys for nothing... and we still play in yellow and blue.

WE WERE VERY successful from early days, especially at minor and junior level. We got to a junior hurling final in our first year and were beaten by Treaty Gaels, a club made up of lads from Limerick.

They had a few illegal players, which wasn't uncommon in those days.

That was the only game we lost in three years. We won the Corn Céitinn Cup in our third year which was a great achievement in those days. The Corn Céitinn was the third most important hurling competition in Dublin.

We played New Irelands in the final in Parnell Park. They were senior champions, but were eligible to play in this competition. It was a marvellous game and finished in a draw. Vinnie Bell scored the equalising point from a sideline cut with the last puck of the game… my first experience of a point scored from a sideline cut.

The replay was fixed for Islandbridge. One of the problems we had in those early days was the dual player issue, and this led to lots of conflicts when it came to fixtures. I was the delegate to the county board and I had been informed by my club not to agree to a re-fixture date… unless we had all our players.

Dominic Bohan was chairman of the Junior Hurling Board and wasn't one bit impressed by our reluctance to play without some of our players. The game was eventually played, and again, it was a fantastic game which we won by a point.

Who else scored that point… but the great Vinnie Bell.

With time running out, Vinnie got the ball and headed down the right wing. We were all wondering where he was going?

But he swept the ball over from an acute angle for an amazing point. It was a significant win for a young club.

Vinnie was an outstanding hurler. There was a big crowd in attendance. Seán McCabe, who was the secretary of the Junior Hurling Board, told me later that they took in £900 at the gate.

One shilling was the admission cost for the game.

So, that tells you how big the crowd was! We celebrated that night in The Milk Bar. The only drink was milk and, if you were a heavy drinker… you got Cidona.

WE WERE PLAYING Scoil Uí Chonaill one evening and our goalie couldn't play, so I was *told* I was to play in goal. I was not impressed, but I had no choice.

I never played outfield after that.

In football, I played as a forward. I was on the 1955 Dublin senior football panel. I played a couple of matches in the O'Byrne Cup. And I was a sub for the championship semi-final versus Mayo, which was a draw.

I was also a sub for the All-Ireland final against Kerry, which we were supposed to win but Kerry were the better team on the day and won 0-12 to 1-6.

I won a Brendan Cup medal against New York, and I played most of the 1956 National League matches, but I played my last football game in 1957. I then decided to focus on hurling.

Tom Young was in the British Army for a few years and then he joined the Palestinian police. He packed that in and came home, and he managed the Na Fianna senior hurling team. He was brilliant with us, but Tom had no time for anyone who didn't get stuck in.

We were playing one very *testy* hurling match and we had a player who was a brilliant hurler, but very timid.

So Tom spoke to him!

'Before the start of the match… I want you pull across your marker. Let him know that you are there!'

'Oh… I couldn't do that, Mr Young!' came the reply.

'In that case, you're not starting today!' announced Tom.

THE TIME HAD come to secure a home base.

We looked around, but land in our area was very difficult to come by.

Home Farm had Mobhi Road, before we got it. Brendan Menton was the key man with Home Farm. He was an out-and-out gentleman.

In due time, the venue was advertised for rent. We made a reasonable offer and we got it, much to our delight. It was, however, in no way fit to play games on. There was a big slope on the main pitch down towards the gate.

We put up goalposts, but they were cut down by somebody… not by Home Farm supporters, by the way, as we were good friends with them.

There was a hut just inside the main gate. It was actually a pig-sty at one time. Seán O'Neill and his father converted this to two small dressing-rooms. Jack Murphy added an outside tap. It was very hard to raise money in those days, so we let the pitch out to a sheep farmer from Monday to Saturday.

This arrangement didn't last too long, as the sheep droppings were all over the pitch and it was unsatisfactory. We converted one area to a pitch and putt course… which made us some revenue.

In 1969, Seán Clerkin became chairman and he transformed the whole club. He was a wonderful man with a big vision, and no challenge was too great. He saw in an advertisement in the paper that the Iveagh Grounds were selling their pavilion.

We got a loan from the Dublin County Board and we purchased it.

Bennie Connolly organised to disassemble it by day, and club volunteers brought it to Mobhi Road at night after they had finished their day's work. We had lots of carpenters in the club and they were more than delighted to do their bit.

It was a fairly sizeable space, but not big enough for dressing-rooms.

We got a quotation of €1600 for a maple floor.

I knew Des McKane, chief executive of Brounskregor. Their business was supplying maple floorboards for bowling alleys. I was chatting to Des one day and I had mentioned to him that we were trying to get a maple floor for our pavilion, but that it was well beyond our capacity to pay.

He informed me that they had lots of off-cuts and we were welcome to them, if we could organise the transport. Again, our great volunteers got moving and collected them, and laid a floor that would have cost £1600 if purchased new. We reckon it cost us around £15.

All the electrical, plumbing and carpentry was done voluntarily by club members.

It was supposed to be officially opened on July 1, 1969, but the night before, there was a break-in... it was set on fire! The story is that the trespasser was looking for drink and when he couldn't find any, he decided to burn down the building. Needless to say, we were shattered.

I got a phone call at 2am and, when I got there, some of the members were already there and suffice to say... if they got their hands on the culprit, he would have been in big trouble.

The police got him subsequently. And he received a 12-month suspended sentence.

We had it insured for about €2,000, which meant it was under-insured.

The Thursday before the fire, the insurance was discussed at a club meeting and Vinny Bell, the acting secretary, proposed that we should increase the value to £9,000. Of course, the chat around Glasnevin was that the fire was an inside job.

SEÁN CLERKIN ORGANISED to have the pitch levelled.

David Hickey's father, Paddy was an engineer with the South of Ireland Asphalt Company, and did all the engineering work. We had a wonderful groundsman in Frank O Flynn from Oldtown.

Seán rang my wife Gretta and told her they were starting camogie in the club and he wanted her to head it up. Now, Gretta never had a camogie stick in her hand in her life. But you just couldn't refuse Seán Clerkin. She organised friends of hers to come on board with her and in their first year they won a Junior A Championship.

We have a hugely successful camogie section now.

Then Seán reintroduced handball to the club. Handball was played one-time down in Green Street, just beside the Law Courts. He also got ladies football going in the club. Then he got rounders up and running.

Seán loved ceili music too, and before long the club was running very successful ceilis every weekend. These nights were extremely popular and were sell-outs. Saturday night was old folks' dance night – again a wonderful success.

The club was being used by the community for choirs, dramatic societies and all sorts of functions. We really were at the service of the local community which was a wish of the founders of the club.

Next, Seán suggested that we needed two full-time workers in the club. We told him we didn't have the money… but he said, 'We'll raise it!'

So we held carnivals in Finglas.

My brother-in-law Mossie Fitzgerald was always looking for angles to make money for the club. He was an engineer in the post office. There were taxes on dances in those days. We had about five carnivals in Finglas. While we made lots of money, we also had lots of hassle.

There was a group of locals there who would come in during the evening and refuse to pay for any rides they went on.

Needless to say, we were very unhappy about that. So Tom Fitzpatrick organised about 20 lads from the club to be there to try to manage the situation. The gang from Finglas arrived with their leader and, when the chair-o-planes stopped, this gang all jumped on and took over a chair each.

The leader was telling his gang not to pay, so Mick Kennedy grabbed him by the shirt and threatened him… and pulled him out of the chair and threw him on the ground. We couldn't believe our eyes, as Mick was such a quiet man.

That solved that problem. Gretta and her friend Angie Collins were selling ice cream in a little booth and these gurriers were pushing it around, even though the two ladies were inside. So, one of our lads produced a hurley… and they fled very fast.

The dodgems belonged to Currys from Derry. Mrs Curry was a lovely lady, but was tough when it came to money.

We also delivered local newspapers in Clontarf.

We tried *everything* to raise money. We are delighted with the club we have now, but it would not have been possible were it not for the commitment of so many people, and all of those wonderful, though at times, scary adventures in the earliest days!

WE ARE VERY strong in hurling now and are winning minor and under-21 titles fairly often. Last year (2021) we reached our first Senior Championship final and, after a great performance, we were very unlucky to lose to Kilmacud Crokes. We have a wonderful young team, and I firmly believe that they will bring the coveted senior hurling championship to Mobhi Road very soon.

We got better and better at football, and won our first senior title in 1969… and we have won four more since. We are very strong at underage and minor level, and more senior titles are not far off hopefully.

Our senior camogie teams have won league titles and a championship should not be far off. The senior ladies footballers have won their share of championships and continue to be one of the leading teams in the county.

◄ ◄ ◆ ▷ ►

GRETTA GRAY

FAST-FORWARD TO 1969.

Na Fianna was the usual GAA Club… men only.

The females of the species had a loose connection – going to matches, supplying tea and sandwiches for visiting teams, washing jerseys, fund-raising, making items for the Annual Sale of Work… but we were not full club members.

All that changed in October that year, as the then chairman of the club, the late Seán Clerkin, a man with an eye to the future, and a pioneer in many ways, decided that the club needed to move forward… and include ladies as full members, and start a camogie section.

I received a phone call from Seán explaining his ideas and inviting me to a meeting in St Vincent's Secondary School. I must say I laughed, and told him I knew nothing about camogie and would only be good for carrying the water bottles. But I agreed to go along.

Most attending the meeting were wives, daughters or sisters of the members of Na Fianna and the outcome, after a lot of discussion, was that I found myself chairwoman of camogie in the club. Eleanor O'Neill was vice-chairwoman (actually, it was either chairwoman or chairperson).

Thus, I found myself at the age of 38, beginning my camogie career and the rest, as they say, is history.

We went to a meeting of the Dublin Camogie Board and were asked why we needed a new club, as there were many clubs we could join. Eventually, they accepted our entry as a junior A camogie team.

We registered our colours, blue and yellow.

In those days, the uniform was a gym-slip, so anyone who could use a sewing machine was roped in and the gym slips came into being – three box pleats front and back, and buttoned on the shoulders, the end trimmed with yellow and tied in the middle with a yellow sash.

Some were better made than others.

This was worn with a white blouse, thick black tights and boots – some wore football boots, and some hockey boots. Mine were hockey boots… and they are hanging in the garage still!

As I had never played camogie before, I decided I had to know what it was all about, so I went training and read the rule book from cover to cover.

They say if you can't beat them, join them, and that is what I did when I took on camogie in Na Fianna, and I did it again when I became secretary of the club, a position I held for four years.

And, once again when I became chairperson of the Dublin Camogie Board for another four year stint.

◂◃◆▹▸

IN MORE RECENT years the biggest addition to the club has been the nursery. In the earlier years, the local schools supplied a lot of our young players.

We live in different times now, and schools have extra pressures and all games have to be promoted. God be good to Brothers O'Farrell, Maher and Kearney.

They introduced so many kids to Na Fianna. It would do your heart good to go to the club on a Saturday morning now and see the number of children from four years of age upwards, and they being coached by coaches and parents.

It is a win-win situation as the kids love it, and the parents are delighted to get them out on a Saturday morning… and, of course, the club benefits big-time.

No wonder we have been so successful at all underage levels in all sports.

Scoil Chaitríona was based in Eccles Street and when the Mater Hospital took over that site, Scoil Chaitríona had to look for other suitable accommodation. They had their eye on Mobhi Road, and they made great efforts to get it (the school moved in 1970). The club got a notice from the Board of Works saying that they would have to vacate Mobhi Road by a certain date. There was consternation, needless to say.

We were just recovering from the burning of our pavilion and Seán Clerkin had come in as chairman with lots of great ideas to move the club forward. My father was involved with Fianna Fáil and Kevin Boland, the minister for Local Government, was a friend of his. So we went to meet him and told him the story.

He told us it was not his department really and the Board of Works didn't come under his jurisdiction, but under the Department of Finance where Charlie Haughey was minister. 'You know,' he said, 'myself and Charlie don't get on, but explain your problem to him. If he doesn't help you I will block it at 'planning'.

There was no Bord Pleanála then and all that area was covered by Local Government.

So we headed down to the Government Offices.

My father knew the run of the place well, so we headed up to Charlie's office. Dad knocked on the door and walked straight in. There was Charlie in a huge office looking through drawers.

'How are you Tommy?' he said.

My dad introduced me to Charlie, whom he referred to as Minister. So, I began to tell Charlie our problem. While I was telling my story, Charlie was still looking through drawers and I got the impression that he wasn't paying attention.

So, my father said to him, 'For f*** sake Charlie, will you look up and pay attention!'

It ended well, as Charlie Haughey wrote to the Board of Works and told them that we were to be accommodated in Mobhi Road. We had a second pitch… and Scoil Chaitríona got that.

However, it's an ill-wind that does no good, as we have a wonderful relationship with the school. We share our facilities and it is very much a win-win situation. But at the time, we didn't feel that way.

And to add to the irony of it all, my daughter Carmel is now principal of the school.

In May 2019, Na Fianna published the ground-breaking report… The social value of CLG Na Fianna.

The study and report were jointly commissioned by the club and the Dublin County Board and followed eight months of extensive research and consultation by Sandra Velthuis of Whitebarn Consulting. The study was carried out following the threat to the club from the construction of Metro North, which would have seen the Mobhi Road GAA facilities put out of commission for up to a decade.

The study was an attempt to put a figure on the social return from the investment in the club. The findings were eye-opening, but at the same time were no huge surprise to people who have been involved in the GAA in Dublin over time. It was found that Na Fianna generated in the order of €50million of social value per year.

For every €1 or equivalent invested in Na Fianna, in the region of €15 of social value was created. When these results are extrapolated to all 91 clubs under the remit of the County Board, the amount of social value generated each year is around €1billion.

This is an extraordinary figure.

All clubs are to be congratulated on their contribution to the communities in their area. We are very grateful to John Costello and the Dublin County Board for their support.

I have a huge belief in Na Fianna, the club of which I am a founder member and through it came my involvement in the wider GAA. I have always believed that a stable society starts with the family, and then with the community.

Dublin has a population of 1.5 million, and the parish rule doesn't really apply in Dublin. Clubs like Na Fianna and many others promote a spirit of co-operation and well-being… we give people somewhere special to belong! We are blessed to have members from all parts of Ireland in our club. They all have played their part in making Na Fianna the club it is today.

Seán O Laoire is one such member. Seán, a great Clareman, worked in Croke Park for many years and has played many active parts in our club, as has his wife Áine. I asked Seán to put on paper some of his reflections on life and on our club.

SEÁN O LAOIRE

The club was founded in 1955 and 60 years later, the Na Fianna club would be viewed as a 'babe in arms' in comparison to the vast majority of GAA clubs, many of whom were founded during the first 20 or 30 years of the association's history. The general structure and make up of GAA clubs affiliated to the Dublin County Board in the 1950s was much different to the units that exist today.

In those years there were fewer community and region-associated clubs. They were, in the main, made up of groups of people who came together through work association. A good example of this would be clubs such as Civil Service, New Irelands, Grocers, Colmcille Kickhams and Young Irelands.

There were also many local and regional based clubs like St Vincent's, St Margaret's, and O'Toole's.

Around this period, and in the following decades, Dublin GAA clubs established strong area and community links which developed and set down roots in a specific region. Good examples of this are clubs like Ballyboden St Enda's, Kilmacud Crokes, Whitehall Colmcille's and many others. Established in an area with strong connections to local schools, these GAA clubs developed and expanded, while creating a strong community-based ethos.

Today, many of these clubs can be categorised as super-clubs. The huge volunteering effort copper-fastened the unique community aspect of these units.

Jimmy Gray and his family were founder members of the Na Fianna club. His ability as an inter-county player was only surpassed by his great dedication and courageous ability as a volunteer administrator. His guiding hand at local level in the club was constant and awe-inspiring.

There were and are very many highlights and indeed some rather devastating low points throughout the life of Na Fianna. Jimmy's guiding hand and wise counsel has helped in no small way throughout this epic journey.

The loss of our pavilion through fire was a major setback. Within a number of years however courage and foresight prevailed and a new clubhouse, Áras Na Fianna was built. 'This modern and unique clubhouse contained many special features, which included team dressing-rooms, a 60 x 30 handball alley with double viewing gallery and spectator seating, a community hall, committee rooms… and a bar and lounge.

Na Fianna was the first GAA club to include a members' bar.

The hall and alley were so designed to allow for multi-use. Over the years, the Saturday night social, the Tuesday night monster bingo, and the long running Sunday night Céilí helped to maximise the use of the wonderful facilities.

The Áras hosted the Special GAA Congress of 1972 which took place in order to consider and discuss far-reaching proposals arising from the McNamee Commission Report. Several Dublin County Board conventions were also held at Mobhi Road.

Ongoing club development has seen the upgrading and extension of the clubhouse to include a much utilised gym for the members, a club shop, a kitchen and dining lounge, and an on-site repair and hurley maker. A pitch side tea/coffee making facility caters for the many adults who attend the successful Saturday morning nursery

Additional to fine playing pitches at Mobhi Road, the hard working facilities committee is occupied cutting and sustaining all these pitches. There are two beautiful all-weather pitches, fully enclosed and featuring a ball-wall beside the clubhouse. There is also a unique specially fitted-out room which hosts, 'Experience Gaelic Games'… a special enterprise which introduces gaelic games to overseas visitors, and tourists and student groups.

The range of club activities is enormous. The playing population is involved in gaelic football, hurling, camogie, handball, ladies football and rounders. The number of teams is over 190. Additional activities include a very popular traditional night which includes Comhrá Gaeilge, which intersperses with music, song and lots of fun.

The report from the Metro North feasibility plan some years ago threw up a 'doomsday scenario' for the club. A bolt from the blue, with no prior notice or consultation, the plan in essence involved the construction of a new Metro system from Phibsboro to Swords via Dublin Airport.

It was planned that a substantial section of the Metro Line would go under-ground. It was planned that two open working tunnels would be sited in such a way that the whole Mobhi Road playing pitch would effectively be a building site for the duration of the project.

This news was a major shock to the members.

It was clearly evident that this project would have serious and far-reaching consequences for the whole community. The whole nation was rather taken aback by the suddenness, the far-reaching consequences and the complete lack of any form of prior notice or consultation.

The matter was raised and discussed by the Government. Apart from the total disbelief and aftershock as the news set in, nobody could estimate the time-scale of the duration of these works.

This announcement unified and galvanised the club as never before.

Each and every member rowed in behind the cause.

A co-operative compelling response which required diligence and dedication was prepared. The membership was motivated and united as never before.

Quality submissions were made and further to a seemingly endless wait, notification came through that an alternative area and site was being considered.

The clarity of focus brought about by this shock, focussed the minds and very soul of the community.

There is little doubt that were the Metro Project to proceed as planned, it would have been the death-knell of the Na Fianna club and the vibrant, inclusive Glasnevin area community.

Players from the club have represented Dublin county teams in all codes on a consistent basis from the foundation of the club. The club honoured all these players on the occasion of the 50th anniversary celebration of our founding in 1955.

A Wall of Fame has been erected in the club reception area, where all the past and present country players are fittingly honoured

Each and every member and friend of Na Fianna was extremely proud and indeed singularly honoured when club member John Horan was elected the 39th president of the Gaelic Athletic Association. John was involved in the club as a player, a team selector, coach, manager and administrator from his youth.

A leader of people and a significant visionary, his list of achievements in the GAA world are forward seeing, positive and inclusive.

His patient approach and task-focussed policies brought to fruition several significant projects during his presidential term in office.

His leadership qualities were never more urgently needed by the GAA, and the country as a whole, as the dreadful Covid 19 pandemic hit the last year of his presidency.

His leadership in that period was immense.

We all, as proud Na Fianna members, are extremely grateful to John.

◄◄◆▷►

Jimmy and his late brother Dinny, photographed at a family wedding, were both instrumental in building up Na Fianna GAA club in its formative years. Many more outstanding men and women have followed in their footsteps helping the club prosper. Enjoying victory in the 2000 Dublin senior football final over Kilmacud Crokes are (inset) Mick Galvin, Dessie Farrell and Kieran McGeeney, while Paul Caffrey managed that brilliant team.

« CHAPTER 3 »

The Challenging 60s

IN THE 10-YEAR period, from 1961 to '71, the population of Dublin grew by 133,887... from 718,332 to 852,219. By 1971, 52% of the population of Ireland was living in urban settlements.

Dublin was now a place of suburban dwellers and this had massive implications for the GAA in Dublin.

It also had implications for the Catholic Church, and 24 new parishes were founded.

Often, the church building was a temporary one and in due time schools followed, and the various amenities that helped make a community. GAA clubs learned early on the benefits of linking with local schools.

MANY NEW CLUBS were founded in the 60s – Clontarf, St Patrick's Palmerstown, Cuala Casements, Dalkey Mitchels, St Monica's, Edenmore, Robert Emmets, Walkinstown Upper, and An Caisleán Drimnagh Castle CBS.

There were also some amalgamations during the same period.

Crumlin, from St Columba's and St Agnes.

Ballyboden St Enda's, from Rathfarnam St Enda's and Ballyboden Wanderers.

Kilmacud Crokes from Crokes and Kilmacud.

Clanna Gael Fontenoy from Clanna Gael and Fontenoy's.

Whitehall Colmcille, from Colmcille and Whitehall Gaels.

The Dublin County Board was now promoting clubs with a strong community base.

There was little or no support for clubs who played for the enjoyment, but had no home base. Ted Cooling, who was secretary of the Dublin County Board, told the annual convention in 1964 that, 'Too many clubs are still content to carry on without a ground. There is no place for such clubs in senior ranks… possibly the hurler on the ditch will be always with us, but the hurler on the ditch belongs to an era long past!'

Commercials and Faughs decided to move out and build a base. Rathcoole became the home for Commercials and Faughs moved to Templeogue. In both cases, these were very wise moves and both clubs have prospered ever since.

On the other hand, a lot of clubs simply disbanded. Westerns, Banba and Geraldine's, just to mention a few, failed to survive.

A few factors accelerated this situation. The changes in the licensing laws for Sunday trading meant that barmen had difficulty in 'getting time off' to play. The introduction of the five-day working week meant that lads from the country could get back to their home clubs for Sunday. Also, more and more cars were on the roads, making it easier to travel home.

It is hard to believe that over 300 clubs disbanded in Dublin since the early days. A lot of these were either institutional or occupational clubs. Some survived for a while, often depending on a car-load of players from some other part of the country.

There are numerous stories in Dublin folklore now of 'bangers'.

A FRIEND OF mine was playing for a junior club on the southside.

They had a game on Sunday morning in Hibernian Park, which was at the top of the Long Mile Road. He was asked by the team manager to stand on the road outside the Red Cow pub and to expect a car to stop and ask for directions. When this car arrived, it had five young healthy-looking men. The driver enquired where was Hibernian Park?

Shortly afterwards, another car arrived again… with five more hurlers inside. They were going to the same venue. As it happened, the first car-load was playing for the opposition. My friend said to me that if he knew that, he would have directed them to a pitch somewhere on the northside.

Another acquaintance of mine was a young Christian Brother in the training college in Marino. A new club was getting off the ground about 10 miles from Marino, but they were always short of hurlers. So the manager would call to the training college on most Sundays looking for a few Brothers who would like a game.

One day my friend asked, 'How many do you want?'

'Eight or nine!' he replied.

THERE WAS ALSO a particular club game in the Fifteen acres in the Phoenix Park on a Sunday morning. The game was fairly close in the first-half and could have gone either way. However, at the start of the second-half a No.17 appeared... and he proceeded to score 3-3 in about 10 minutes or so. The losing manager was not impressed and had his suspicions. At the end of the game he asked the referee to get the name of No.17. However, the manager of the winning team instructed his team to go straight to the dressing-rooms.

When the referee got to the winning dressing-room he asked to see the player wearing the No 17 jersey. A young local lad stood up, definitely not the player who scored 3-3 in 10 minutes.

Seán O'Neill, our club official, would have you expelled if you played an over-age player or a banger. One Sunday morning, back in the Phoenix Park, we were playing and at the end of the game the manager of the losing team came and informed us that we had a banger on board.

We said that we hadn't, and we asked him what evidence had he? He named one of our players, and said he had already played a game for their club the previous day. When we challenged the player, his only answer was, 'They asked me to play... I only wanted a game!' Clubs like Fr Murphy's, Commercials and Grocers were just one-team clubs and they had no base. Faughs were different, and Tommy Moore, their boss, was very strict and insisted on playing by the rules.

Lucan Sarsfields were in a Junior C final against Fr Murphy's in the early-70s. Two of the Fr Murphy's team were members of the 1968 Wexford senior hurling team that defeated Tipperary in the All-Ireland final. There was an objection to the result. Now, Dublin clubs didn't normally object to bangers, but bringing in two All-Ireland medal winners was a bit much.

The Dublin Board heard the objection and gave the two players a 12-month suspension each. The Wexford Board were upset by Dublin's decision to suspend two of their players and they appealed to the Leinster Council. One witness, a priest from Kilmuckridge, said that he saw the two players at his 11.0 Mass that morning. Another witness, a waiter from the Talbot Hotel, said that he served them breakfast that morning. They still lost the appeal.

However, they brought their case to Croke Park and had the suspension lifted. The great John Doyle is reported as saying that these two lads were only helping the promotion of hurling in Dublin and, for that reason, they should not be punished.

ONE OF OUR first finals was in O'Toole Park against Treaty Gaels.

I was sitting with Seán O'Neill in the dressing-room before the game. These two lads arrived in and sat down beside us. One of them asked us, 'Well lads, what's the opposition like?'

We said, 'Who is the opposition?'

And he replied, 'Na Fianna!'

They were in the wrong dressing-room and they had come up from Limerick for the day. Dublin clubs very rarely objected to bangers as they understood the difficulty some clubs had in getting 15 players to make up a team.

Other changes that all institutions had to adjust to included the introduction of free secondary education in 1967 and, before that, RTE providing a national television service from 1961. As well as the reduction of the working week, statutory holidays became law. The World Cup final in Wembley in 1966 made soccer a very attractive sport, and the GAA could never again expect full allegiance from all Irishmen.

The Dublin County Board appreciated the new world they were living in, and Tom Loftus, the Dublin Chairman, set up a special committee to look at eight different aspects that needed attention.

Aspects 7 and 8 caused some contention. These were:

7. To inquire into and report on the present administrative arrangements and to recommend what steps, if any, appear necessary to secure greater efficiency in administration.

8. To inquire into and report on, and make any recommendations considered necessary on such other matters as are, in the opinion of the committee, related to, or arising out of the foregoing.

DR JJ Stuart, affiliated to UCD and a former president of the GAA was appointed chairman. The committee issued a questionnaire to all clubs and reported back to Dublin County Board one year later. Some of the findings of the report included:

• Football was much more popular than hurling.

• In 1963 there were 181 clubs affiliated compared to 90 in 1938.

• The number of teams participating in 1963 was 717 compared to 330 in 1938.

• The biggest jump in numbers was in the minor and juvenile grades. The Juvenile Leagues had 21 teams in football and eight in hurling in 1938. Twenty-five years later the numbers were up to 126 football teams and 91 hurling teams.

• The running of the senior hurling and football championships was described as 'chaotic'. Finals were often delayed for months, sometimes because some clubs were unable to field teams during the summer months.

The committee recommended that all championships should finish by the summer break and the league should run from September to April.

The most controversial proposal was the establishment of a joint Hurling and Football League Committee to manage the running of the leagues and cup competitions, amongst other things.

Discipline was a major issue and the committee recommended setting up a group of five people to deal with this area.

It took two years before the recommendations were dealt with at a special convention and the proposed new management structure did not get the necessary two-thirds majority and so it failed.

DUBLIN'S GREATEST CHALLENGE going forward was how to deal with the new centres of population and, more especially, to get land to develop playing pitches. Just when clubs were planning new clubhouses and playing facilities, building costs were soaring and finance was an issue for all clubs. The playing of more inter-county games in Croke Park was affecting club support and gates.

The 'community' idea caught on from the mid-60s.

Previously, the GAA saw its remit as the organisation and playing of games. Séamus Ó Riain was president of the GAA from 1967 to '70 and he set up a scheme where clubs could avail of grants to carry out ground development. Ciste na Banban was set up by the Cork Board and it ran weekly draws where clubs that partook could get a percentage back for their development.

Dublin clubs accepted the need to cater for wives and families, as well as players, and they started the process of upgrading and building clubhouses, in addition to proper dressing-rooms. Inisfail purchased land from a local landowner and opened their pavilion in 1967 with a challenge match between Dublin and Roscommon. O'Dwyer's moved to a new pitch with floodlights and dressing-rooms. Erin's Isle had to deal with disputes and compulsory purchase order issues before opening their new facilities in Farnam Road. St Vincent's opened their new grounds in Raheny in 1963. Kilmacud opened their Glenalbyn Community Centre in 1966.

My own club, Na Fianna, moved to Mobhi Road and development of other facilities started immediately. In all these developments, voluntary labour was critical and club members were not found wanting.

Looking back now, I must give credit to all involved in making the appropriate adjustments to cater for the 'new' situation. Nobody could have foreseen the massive population growth and its implications for all.

I am very proud of how the GAA dealt with the challenge.

Jimmy and Gretta walking down O'Connell Street in 1958, the year before their marriage. And (below) with their children John and Tom, and Carmel and Annmarie in the 70s.

« CHAPTER 4 »

Days in Blue

PADDY LILLIS FROM St Vincent's was the Dublin goalie before me, and he was a good one. I was picked for a game when Dublin played the Army in a charity match in Newbridge as Paddy wasn't available. That was my debut for Dublin.

I broke my finger playing for Na Fianna and so that ruled me out for a few months. My first real game for Dublin was in 1958, in a National League game versus Kilkenny played at O'Toole Park. Paddy Croke was right corner-back and Seán Clohosey's brother Timmy, who was the chief executive at Switzers department store, was playing corner-forward for Kilkenny.

Timmy was a very fast player and as he ran past Paddy he got a clatter in the hand. He said to Paddy, 'What did you do that for?'

'You hardly expected me to let you go through for a goal did you?' came the reply.

'I suppose you're right!' says Timmy.

We played Kilkenny in the Leinster final in Croke Park in 1959. We were two points up with five minutes of injury time gone. Jack Conroy, God be good to him, was doing umpire, and he said to me, 'Jimmy, ye are all right, ye have it… well done!'

Johnny McGovern cut a sideline from the corner. It landed in the square, and Seán Clohosey pulled on it… and into the back of the net! We lost by a point.

That was a really good team we had that year. Kilkenny went on to play

Waterford in the final, but lost in a replay. Our first two games in the league were against Kilkenny, who we beat in Croke Park, and Waterford the following Sunday. We won that one too. In 1960, we played Wexford in the first round of the championship at Nowlan Park…we lost by four points.

I had to go off when I got a knock on the head from Tom Ryan, I think. Willie Jackson went in to goal and spent the rest of the match looking for an opportunity to get a crack at the culprit. Again, we had a really good team and, with a bit of luck, could have won two finals. However, it was not to be. Wexford went on to win the All-Ireland that year.

LATER THAT YEAR, we played Cork, down in Cork. That was the first time I came up against Christy Ring. There was a schemozzle around the square and, as the ball was going over the bar, Christy stuck me in the back of the net with a shoulder.

Years afterwards… Eithne Haughey, Charlie's sister, was a receptionist at our office and she called me one day.

'There is a gentleman here who wants to see you,' she told me. 'I don't know who he is!' she added.

General Costello was my boss and I was only new to the job, so I didn't want to be away from my desk without a good reason. But I went down to reception and who was there but the bold Christy Ring. He was sitting down with a young lady beside him. I asked him what he was doing here, and he told me that the young lady was his niece… and she had applied for a job in Erin Foods.

It was a very good job as demonstrator, with a company car going with it. Christy felt it would enhance her chances if he came along with her. I had no say in deciding who would get the job, but I wished her the best of luck and went back to my office.

I was just sitting down in my chair, when the door burst open and in walked Christy. 'Listen Jimmy!' he said, 'That young lassie of mine is the best candidate for that job and you better make sure she gets it… and don't forget that lesson I taught you years ago in Cork!'

Again, I reminded him I was only a few months in the job myself, so I had no say in the appointment of staff. She actually got the job but, for some reason, didn't take it.

IN 1961, WE did well in the league. We played both Limerick and Antrim at their home venues. Limerick and Antrim were struggling at that time and it was agreed to give them more home matches so as to promote the game. Our first championship match was against Westmeath in Tullamore.

Even though we won by 10 points we really didn't play well. We then met Wexford in Kilkenny in the Leinster final. It was a wonderful game, which we won on a score of 7-5 to 4-8. Noel Drumgoole, our full-back, kept Andy Doyle scoreless. Andy had scored 4-3 in the previous game against Kilkenny. Noel was a wonderful hurler and when he got a job to do... he always did it. Andy was a fine hurler, in the Nickey Rackard mould, and took serious watching. Noel got the Man of the Match award that day. I'm told that was one of my best days in goal for Dublin.

A funny incident happened on the way home from the game.

A few former players like Jim Prior and Ned Dunphy joined us on the bus on the return journey to Dublin. When we reached Castledermot, they suggested we stop for 'one drink'. This was about eleven o'clock now, and the players just wanted to get home and rest... and get ready for work on Monday.

Ned and Jim knew the owner of one of the pubs... they were sure they would get in. When they knocked on the door, the owner peeped out and said she could not let them in as there was a new guard in town and all the pubs were under surveillance.

'Actually,' she said, 'he is up there on the bridge looking down at us now. If you want to go and ask him that is okay with me.'

So the two boys got the Bob O'Keeffe Cup and went up to talk to the guard. They explained that they had won the Leinster final and they just wanted one pint to celebrate. The guard was having none of it and, in spite of many requests, he didn't change his mind.

When the lads knew that there was no point in continuing the argument, Ned said to the guard, 'You know what guard, I'd love to f**k you over that bridge... into the river!'

When they came back to the bus they were very uncomplimentary of every guard in the country. They were two great characters. Jim was centre-back for Dublin when they lost to Cork in the 1952 All-Ireland final. He was an extraordinary hurler. He was a Tipperary man but in spite of many requests to go back and play for Tipp, he remained loyal to Dublin, unlike so many others. He could also drink for Ireland.

I was leaving O'Toole Park one day after a game and I offered Jim a lift home. He said he wanted to go to the hospital. I asked why the hospital and he answered, 'It can cure every problem I have.'

When I reached the Mater Hospital, I stopped.

Jim told me to keep going! He said he would tell me when to stop.

We eventually stopped outside a favourite pub of his. 'This is not a hospital, Jim!'

'No!' he replied, 'But it has a cure for my problem.'

SO, WE WERE now in the All-Ireland final.

We really should have won the game. We had a poor start, but we had a wonderful second-half and a lot of neutrals would say that we were the better team on the day even though Tipperary were hot favourites. Tipperary were given a point when it was well, well wide. The umpire was a Down man and I challenged him, but to no avail. Lar Foley and myself would rotate the puckouts, and Lar took the next puckout… and brought the hurley well back in the hope of making contact with the umpire.

Lar got sent off later on. Tom Ryan pulled on a ball and hit Snitchy Ferguson by accident. Lar wasn't impressed and clattered Tom… both got sent off. Noel Drumgoole would keep an eye on Lar during the game and would be constantly saying, 'Shut up, Lar!'

I could write another book about Lar, if I could only remember half of the stories. We could have won that game, but we didn't really believe it. Tipperary were a great team at the time and we probably had an inferiority complex going in to that game.

The match reports were very complimentary and said that Dublin hurling had a bright future. We are still waiting for the big day to come… when we win the Liam MacCarthy Cup. 2013 was our best chance and we were so unlucky to lose to Cork, who lost to Clare in the final.

I believe we would have beaten Clare as we owed them one after losing to them in 2012.

This is the report of our defeat to Tipp in 1961, from *The Irish Times*.

‹ ‹ ◆ ▷ ►

TIPPERARY WINS BUT GLORY BELONGS TO DUBLIN

by a Staff Reporter

Tipperary 0-16 Dublin 1-12

Tipperary will go into the record books as All-Ireland champions 1961, but in years to come when statistics are the only evidence of mastery in the hurling field, the meagre one point margin by which they won at Croke Park yesterday cannot rob Dublin of the honour and glory they earned so magnificently in this All-Ireland Hurling Final.

They entered the game as rank outsiders. Their Leinster form against Wexford was good, the critics said, but not half good enough to beat a powerful Tipperary side which annihilated Cork in the Munster decider. It looked as if these predictions would be borne out when Tipperary slammed over points within three minutes of the start. It looked as if a jittery, hesitant metropolitan defence would be torn to shreds by the end of the first quarter.

ROT HALTED

But that disastrous opening, bred obviously of fear and nerves, lasted no more than five minutes. The rot was halted with points from Jackson and Shannon in the fifth and sixth minutes and from there on the real tough, determined Dublin emerged. Their defence suddenly tightened.

The tall ranging Des Foley began slowly but surely to exert a midfield dominance that lasted to the end. And a fast attack led cleverly by the Boothman brothers and Jackson probed the Tipperary backs with lightning sorties that promised a spate of scores. That these did not come from the end of the first quarter onwards was due more to a serious flaw in Dublin's midfield than to the covering of the Tipperary backs who apart from Burns and John Doyle were often flurried under pressure.

Des Foley was now playing majestic hurling in the centre of the field but the extraordinary ineptness of his partner Whelan gave Tipperary the breaks they needed and the bespeckled O'Gara took them with coolness and precision. Why Dublin selectors did not switch Whelan with left half-forward Shannon at this stage must remain one of the mysteries of the game.

This move or indeed any move to aid Foley would almost certainly have turned a four point deficit – 0-6 to 0 -10 – into a short Dublin lead at half-time.

Then to add to their misfortune the Dublin backs fouled needlessly and a crack marksman Jimmy Doyle, took four easy points from frees. The big Tipperary following among the 67,836 crowd must have felt happy at the end of the first-half which rarely reached All-Ireland standard. Tipperary were not shaping like champions but neither were Dublin so the experience and toughness of the Munster men would surely tell in the end.

GREAT GOAL

But those Tipperary supporters got the biggest shock of their lives within six minutes of the restart. The Dublin centre half-back sent a long clearance to Shannon who lobbed the ball through to left corner Jackson. The former goalkeeper grabbed it and left Hassett, the Tipperary right full-back, flat-footed and sent the ball whistling to the back of the net.

That goal – the only major score of the game – transformed Dublin and lifted the remaining 24 minutes into the bracket of memorable All-Ireland finals. When A. Boothman brought Dublin level with a point thirty seconds after Jackson's tonic goal Tipperary panicked and those light blue jerseyed hurlers, sensing their big chance, tore into every tussle with a grim abandon. Although the Tipperary forwards were still threatening danger every time they moved up field, the Dublin backs, inspired by a thundering performance from right full Ferguson, were now covering, and blocking and clearing like men possessed.

Des Foley, getting more assistance from midfielder Whelan, was beating the Tipperary midfielders to a frazzle and the Boothmans, Shannon and Jackson were cutting lanes through the opposing defence. When the Dublin men led by two points with only 12 minutes to go it seemed the title must return to the capital for the first time since 1938.

Even when Tipperary took the lead again with a string of three points, Dublin continued to shape like champions. But then came the most ironic twist of the game. Ferguson, who had done so much to earn victory for the City men, picked the ball off the ground on the 21 yards line and Jimmy Doyle pointed an easy free. The Dublin point which followed from Boothman on the twenty fifth minute, would have drawn the match if Ferguson had not lost his head in a situation which could have been easily saved with a first time clearance.

Dublin got two late chances to pull the game out of the fire but Jackson hit the outside of the net with a stinging drive and Shannon misdirected a 40 yards free from the left wing.

18TH TITLE

So Tipperary held on to win their 18th title but Dublin took most of the honours on the day. All through Tipperary were only a shadow of the side that beat Cork. An unfit Tony Wall left a gap at half-back which Dublin saw early and exploited to the full. Nealon was a constant menace to the Dublin defence but Jimmy Doyle, although he claimed the major score of Tipperary's total of nine points – seven from frees – was obviously affected by the ankle injury which kept him out of training.

If Tipperary were so poor, how then did Dublin lose?

There are four reasons: A bad start which gave Tipperary three early points, Whelan's below par performance at midfield, Ferguson's unfortunate infringement six minutes from the end and Devaney's switch to centre half-back when Wall was taken off late in the game. In this vital period, Devaney stemmed several Dublin raids which might easily have been turned into winning scores if Wall, also showing the effects of his recent injury, had been allowed to remain in the game. Two players, Lar Foley and Tom Ryan were sent to the line by referee Fitzgerald after a brief flair up in the Dublin goal midway in the second-half. Apart from this however, the game was free of rancour and incidents.

Tipperary called in three subs, Tom Ryan for McKenna, J Hough for O'Gara and S McLoughlin for Tony Wall. E Malone came on for Bohan on the Dublin team.

Scorers: Tipperary: *J Doyle 0-9, Nealon 0-3, O'Gara 0-2, Tom McLoughney 0-1, McKenna 0-1.* **Dublin:** *A Boothman 0-5, Shannon 0-3, Jackson 1-2, D Foley 0-1, B Boothman 0-1.*

Tipperary: *D O'Brien: M. Hassett (capt), M Maher, K Carey: M Burns, A Wall, John Doyle: M O'Gara, T English: Jimmy Doyle, L Devaney, D Nealon: J McKenna, W Moloughney, T McLoughney.*

Dublin: *J Gray: D Ferguson, N Drumgoole (capt), L Foley; L Ferguson, C Hayes, S Lynch; D Foley, F Whelan; A Boothman, M Bohan, L Shannon; B Boothman, P Croke, W Jackson*

◄ ◄ ◆ ▷ ►

THE DAY AFTER the All-Ireland final, we got a guided tour of Jacob's biscuit factory. Our star forward, Achill Boothman, worked for Jacob's. It is said that he got the job on the proviso he would play soccer for the Jacob's team.

So he played for a few years, but there was never any doubt about his first love. He had extraordinary pace and could strike a ball while running at full speed. Jim Browne, who was a young lad when the Boothmans were in their prime, said that he and a few friends would be at the entrance to Pearse Park and would carry Achill and Bernard's kit bags as they arrived for training.

They would stay behind the goal, while the players were training and the only balls they were interested in were those hit by Achill or Bernard. They lived on Derry Road, and Bernard would be out in the front garden and Achill would be in the back garden… and they would puck the ball over the roof to each other.

Jim said there was always a buzz when certain players got on the ball and one of those players was Achill. He scored five points in the 1961 All-Ireland final. He was an extremely shy man with no self-confidence. Jim asked him once would he come up to the field to coach the young lads and his response was, 'Ah, I'd be no good at that kind of thing!' John Doyle, of Tipperary fame, said in his memoir that Achill was his most difficult opponent. He was a lovely, humble man.

I WAS A sub to Ollie Walsh on a few Railway Cup teams. Ollie was the outstanding goalie of that period, so it was an honour to be his understudy.

One of the years, I was involved… we played Ulster up in Cavan. Billy Rackard was centre-back. We travelled in style in those days in Joe O'Hara's limousines. Ned Wheeler from Wexford was playing midfield. Ulster had two small guys from Antrim also at midfield. They were two narky little 'so and so's' and they were going around clattering fellas. Ned got another belt, so he turned to the offender and said, 'If you do that again… I will do you!' The little lad did it again, of course.

And Ned just knocked him to the ground. He asked his pal to get Ned, but when the pal saw the size of Ned he decided to walk away.

ONE ST PATRICK'S Day, a Rest of Ireland selection played Kilkenny in Thurles. I was sub goalie for the 'Rest'. The following day we played Tipperary and I was in goal. Christy Ring was captain of the Rest of Ireland and he was going around the dressing-room asking for commitment to ensure we defeated Tipp. He came over to me.

'You better deliver today. You know you shouldn't be in goal… it should be Ollie Walsh.' Needless to say, I didn't feel great after those less than inspiring words. We won the game and, as we changed, Christy spoke up again.

'You did okay… but you know Ollie should have been there!'

WE PLAYED TIPPERARY in Wembley one Whit Weekend.

It was a very high scoring game because of the shortened pitch. There was a meal afterwards in Wembley. I had a contact in London and he got three tickets to see *My Fair Lady* in the West End. Gretta loves the theatre, as did Noel Drumgoole.

So, after the meal, I hired a taxi to get us to the theatre. We arrived about 20 minutes late. Our seats were five rows from the front… in the middle. As we moved to our seats, we had to hold our gear bags and hurleys over our heads to avoid hitting anybody.

We must have been some sight.

MY LAST GAME for Dublin was a league match in 1968, in Croke Park.

I was married by then and the kids were young. I had a really good game, but afterwards I decided that I was retiring. I was also very busy at work. I was 37 years of age and even though I wanted to go on, I knew I had no choice. I must admit it was a very difficult decision for me.

Looking back on the 1959 to '63 era I regret that we didn't win an All-Ireland.

We were in four Leinster finals in my time – 1959, '61, '63 and '64. And we only won one. For different reasons we lost Norman Allen, Tony Young and Kevin Heffernan. They would have made a massive difference in 1960 and '61.

Before the 1961 All-Ireland, we played Faughs in a training game and I let in seven goals. I should have saved six of them. Gerry O'Connor, a great character, was a selector and as I walked off the pitch he came over and put his arm around my shoulder.

'Don't worry about that, Jimmy!

'Remember, you always play your best man in goal!' He then handed me a transfer form to sign for his club Eoghan Ruadha. Na Fianna were playing intermediate at the time and Gerry felt I would benefit from playing with a senior club. I stayed with Na Fianna.

Overall, I have wonderful memories and made some great friends.

Tony Wall, who captained Tipp in 1961, is also a member of Clontarf Golf Club. I enjoy meeting players from that era and we have fun reminiscing about the 'good old days'.

◄◄◆►►

DONIE NEALON
(Five-time Tipperary All-Ireland Winner)

We had lost the 1960 final badly. Some army fellow from Limerick was put over us as trainer. Imagine me, a light skinny fella, carrying Mikey Maher around on my back and he after having a few drinks before he arrived.

We didn't start training for the All-Ireland final until the Monday week before. We did five nights in-a-row... and then Monday, Tuesday and Wednesday of the following week. We were absolutely stuck to the ground in Croke Park.

A middling team from Wexford hammered us. We were talked-up as hot favourites to beat Dublin in the 1961 final. But every team is beatable on the day. I used to play for UCD at the time and I knew the Dublin players fairly well, and I also knew that Mick Ryan was a fairly good trainer. We started well and went a few points up. We knew that Tony Wall and Jimmy Doyle were not fully fit but we kept it to ourselves. We still felt we would win, even with two unfit players on the field.

Just before half-time, we had a controversial goal disallowed. The ball came into the square and everybody pulled. There was no putting up your hand in those days. I got a belt on the nose and fell down on the ground. My hurley was gone as well.

Lying on the ground, I opened my eyes and there was the ball about three inches outside the goal-line. I had no hurley... and had a player lying on me, so I shoved the ball over the line with my elbow. The referee and the umpires took a long time talking about it and they eventually disallowed it.

I have a feeling that the ball was over the line and was brought back out by somebody. I could be wrong. I often mentioned it to Jimmy Gray in later years but he never really took the bait. That was a big blow to us and a good let off for Dublin. Just after that,

Mackey McKenna doubled on a ball from about 10 yards out and Snitchy Ferguson stuck out his hurley and deflected it over the bar.

In the second-half Dublin's fitness had us really rattled. The Boothmans and Larry Shannon were flying. Dublin had great backs with Snitchy Ferguson, Noel Drumgoole and Lar Foley in the full-back line. Christy Hayes was an excellent centre-back and, of course, Des Foley at midfield was probably the best centrefield in the country at the time.

He had it every way – size, strength and skill. They began to run us into the ground. They were flying it. They got a well-worked goal and they were back in the game big time. The turning point was when Lar Foley and Tom Ryan got sent off for a very minor altercation. Tom had just come on for Mackey McKenna and I don't think he even touched the ball. Lar going off was a big loss for Dublin, as it opened up their defence.

Tom McLoughney was full-forward and came out, and said to me, 'We are going to lose again!' I won't tell you the language I used, but I told him to get back to his place. Dublin had a great chance of a goal as time was nearly up. It hit the side-netting. We would never have won only for Liam Devanney going back centre-back. He lorded it.

We were just holding on by a point.

Noel Drumgoole got the ball and threw it up to clear it, and Tom McLoughney walked in between the ball and the hurley and took the full blow of the hurley to the body. It kept the ball away from the Dublin forwards, and we held on to win by a point.

We were very lucky to win. It must have been a bitter blow for Dublin as they could have won it. Who knows what would have happened Dublin hurling if they had won that day.

◄◄◆►►

The Dublin team that lost to Tipperary by a single point in the 1961 All-Ireland hurling final.

« CHAPTER 5 »

Refereeing

IT IS HARD to believe now how referees were appointed back in the 60s, and no doubt in the years before that. When fixtures were read out at the Leinster Council meetings, the top table would ask for proposals for referees for all games, except finals.

The executive picked the referees for the finals.

You might have a few proposals, then seconders and a vote would be held to decide the successful candidate. Martin O'Neill was secretary of the Leinster Council and he ran the show. When it came to the 1969 Leinster hurling final between Offaly and Kilkenny, 'Jemmy Gray' was announced from the top table as the referee.

Martin always called me, 'Jemmy Gray'.

I said, 'Mr Chairman, I have never refereed a senior inter-county game before!'

Martin retorted, 'You'll be alright, both counties have agreed to you!'

Now, I had only refereed a few minor games in Dublin as I was still playing senior club hurling and football myself. I had never done any kind of inter-county game. So, as you can see, it was a different era, and that wouldn't happen now.

NOW, GETTING BACK to the final, there was a rail strike at the time and there was concern that the revenue from gate receipts would be down. Before the throw-in, Paddy Molloy, one of the great Offaly hurlers, said to me as he was passing down to his position, 'Jimmy, you will look after us, won't you?'

Kilkenny only won by two points… 3-9 to 0-16.

Anyway, I did a fairly good job and there were no problems. Both sides played good tough hurling. The fact that I was a player myself, I knew most of the lads from both sides and had played Railway Cup games with some of them.

Later on, I was talking to Martin O'Neill and he said to me, 'Jemmy, you did a very good job, but you made one mistake… you forgot the bloody rail strike.' Needless to say, a draw would have been a better result as the replay would draw a much bigger crowd.

The following year, I refereed Laois and Westmeath in Tullamore in the first round of the Leinster Championship. It was a hardy match, with a fair deal of skelping in it. Two players were hammering the hell out of each other, so I sent them off.

The Laois crowd accepted it.

But Westmeath supporters were incensed. The chairman of Westmeath gave out hell to me for sending the players off. Westmeath's real problem was that their player was a dual player and he would be missing the football game the following Sunday.

When I was coming out of the dressing-room and ready to go home, Tommy Ring, God be good to him, was outside with a few supporters.

When he saw me he said, 'Jimmy the next time we play Na Fianna, I will deal with you'. Tommy was a wonderful Westmeath hurler, and he played his club hurling for Kilmacud Crokes in Dublin. Anyway, when we met in a club game a few weeks later nothing happened. I bumped into Tommy on the way out after the game and I said to him that I was half-expecting he might carry out the threat he made in Tullamore.

'Ah Jimmy,' he said, 'That was said in the heat of the moment… I had no intention of doing anything!' Tommy became a great Dublin supporter for years afterwards and we often met on The Friends of Dublin Hurling buses on the way to Dublin games. His son Conny was a serious hurler for Craobh Chiaráin and for Dublin. His daughter Martina played camogie for Dublin and rarely misses a Dublin game.

I don't think I refereed any more big games as they often clashed with club games for Na Fianna and that always came first with me

I CONTINUED TO referee some club matches.

I refereed a replay final between St Vincent's and Kilmacud Crokes. Des Foley got a broken leg in the first match. I must admit I thought it was an accident. There were all sorts of rumours about the replay and that there may be some revenge for the injury to Des.

Tom Loftus, was the Dublin chairman at the time and, as this game was before the Leinster Championship, he encouraged me not to send off any county players. Anyway, there was no problem in the replay.

At a county board meeting later on a delegate recommended that no referee should be appointed with a view to *not* sending off certain players. That was a reference to me, obviously.

Looking back now, I must say that the arrangements for game officials were very loose. You brought your own linesmen and neutral counties were asked to supply the umpires. There were no 'referee courses' in those days.

Fitness was up to yourself! There was no gear supplied, and you wore whatever colours you had. Despite all of this, I must admit I actually enjoyed refereeing those games.

It was the next best thing to playing yourself.

BILLY GOODISON FROM Wexford was a very good football referee, as was Frank Murphy from Cork for hurling games. Dickie Murphy was a wonderful hurling referee and he knew when to blow and not to blow. I must say, things are much better now.

However, in spite of Hawkeye, and referee evaluations, some referees make big mistakes and teams suffer as a consequence. Without referees, at the same time, we would not have games, so I am totally in favour of supporting referees – human error does occur, and we have to put up with it.

I also agree with the use of Hawkeye for scores. The sliotar is small, the uprights are very high… and on a sunny day you could easily be unsighted. I would not like to see it used for anything else. Watching a bit of soccer now, I feel that VAR is causing more problems than it is solving.

Joseph's football club had some wonderful characters. Phil Grogan, who was known as the 'gurrier', was one such character and a very decent fella – and he came to my rescue one day when I was refereeing a club match out in Swords between Ballyboughal and Fingallians. At half-time a fella came across to me and said, 'Fins better win this match!'

With time running out, I gave a free to Ballyboughal and they won the match with the last kick of the game. Some of the Fingallian supporters were very irate and they surrounded me… calling me a few choice names. I was worried because I was on my own.

Then I heard the shout… 'JIMMY… ARE YOU OKAY?'

And who was it, but Phil.

He came in to the field and escorted me off, and the Fingallian supporters moved away quietly. He was a wonderful character, but I would not like to cross him.

PHIL ALSO CAME to my rescue on a second occasion!

We had a ship coming in to collect some cargo and the captain phoned saying he wanted £140 to pay his staff. So, I was sent down on behalf of the Sugar Company to deliver the money.

When I met him, he said he only wanted £70.

I had £70 left over. On the way home, I was walking up by the North Wall. As I was passing the Point Depot, I was confronted by two boyos who said, 'We know that you have money… hand it over!'

I had no intention of doing that, and I took off like the hammers of hell.

I got as far as Connell's Pub, and Phil happened to be outside the door chatting to a friend. He said to me, 'What the hell's wrong with you?'

I told him my story.

'I'll deal with them!' said Phil, and he headed down toward the Point. I heard the gates rattling so I decided to go down and see what was happening. I met a fella running toward me at 90 miles an hour. Then I saw another fella sitting on the ground holding his jaw.

I said to Phil, 'These are not the guys!'

And Phil said, 'F***ing… so what!'

REFEREEING IS A tough task and, even though I have been known to be hard on them, I do feel for them at times. We played Galway in a league match in Salthill.

We were two points down with time running out. If we won, we would have been in the semi-final. John Dowling of Offaly was the referee. We got a '70' so Lar Foley went up to help the forwards. Des Foley took it, and the referee informed him that he would have to score direct.

The ball fell short… and all hell broke out with players flaking left, right and centre, with Lar doing more than his share. The ball wound up in the back of the net… how it got there was anybody's guess.

John Dowling blew the full-time whistle and ran to the dressing-rooms. Snitchy Ferguson was our captain and he followed John, and asked him was he allowing the goal? John told him to go away, but he reported him in his referee's report for abuse.

Snitchy got suspended.

When we got to the dressing-room a few stones had come in through the window. We went back to the Imperial Hotel in Eyre's Square and there was a huge crowd milling around. Fr O'Dea was chairman of the Galway County Board and he got the crowd to disband. He then came in to the hotel and he apologised profusely for the misconduct of the supporters. When he was finished, Lar piped up, 'Ah don't worry, Father, we will still go to Mass next Sunday'.

Referees are nearly an endangered species and some of them opt out because of the abuse they get. I have been at games and the abuse from the sidelines is totally unacceptable. Clubs need to get tough on this and deal with people whose behaviour is unacceptable.

We must remember… no referees, no games.

Jimmy was thrown into the deep end as a referee, which was normal in the 60s and 70s. John Moloney from Tipperary (above) taking charge of the 1974 All-Ireland hurling final between Limerick and Kilkenny was one of the game's top officials. The modern game, however, is ruled and commanded a bit differently, as shown here (below) when Fergal Horgan posed with his match officials before the 2020 All-Ireland hurling final between Limerick and Waterford.

« CHAPTER 6 »

The County Board

FOR MOST OF my adult life, I have been involved with the Dublin County Board and, I must say, I have enjoyed every minute of it.

Where did it all begin? Tom Fitzpatrick, one of the most extraordinary people I have known, was the real *mover* in the formation of Na Fianna. He was a dictator and he had to be in those days. He informed me I was going to be the club representative to the Dublin Junior Board. This was my introduction to the administrative side of the GAA.

As a delegate to the Junior Board, I got to know the workings of the board itself. I soon realised that the structure of the board was antiquated but I wasn't in any position to do anything about it. When Na Fianna acquired senior status in hurling, I was appointed delegate to the Senior Board. I came in touch with a lot of different people, some enlightened like the great Noel Drumgoole, but the majority were very conservative and were happy just to keep doing things like they always did.

The chairman at the time was Tom Loftus, an excellent officer, but he didn't get the opportunity to take the necessary steps to bring about change.

I felt he had ambitions for higher office and, in due time, he became chairman of the Leinster Council. For some reason or another, he took a shine to me, probably because we had many discussions on where the GAA in Dublin should be going.

I HAD NO ambitions at this stage for promotion. I was satisfied to represent my club… and I was still playing for my club and my county. One night, I was leaving Tom home to his house in Stillorgan, when he said to me, 'You will have to stand for the position of chairman at this year's Dublin convention'.

To say that I was surprised would be an understatement.

I declined at first largely because I had been promoted in the Irish Sugar Company and had to take on much more responsibility. He persisted, so I let my name go forward, but I really felt I had no chance of being elected. Tom's own club, Foxrock Geraldines, proposed me. Arthur Nolan was chairman of the Junior Football Board, which was the largest unit in Dublin GAA, and he would have been considered favourite for the position. Anyway, to my great surprise, I defeated Arthur by 10 votes. It was only then that the enormity of the task ahead dawned on me.

Dublin was the biggest unit in the GAA. General Costello was the boss in the Sugar Company and my first reaction was what would he think. Much to my relief, he rang me to congratulate me. I was very relieved as he was a tough task master.

I told my good wife that the term was only three years. In actual fact, I served 'a little longer' in that position. After the elation of being elected I had to get my thoughts together on how I was going to approach the job.

At that time, Jim King was the honorary secretary and Denis Skehan was the treasurer. They filled me in on how things were run and this confirmed what I had already thought. People were set in their ways and I knew I wasn't going to be very popular if I started making structural changes.

At the time there were seven different boards – Senior Board, Senior Football Board, Senior Hurling Board, Junior Football Board, Junior Hurling Board, Minor Board and the Fingal Board. All very independent, and resistant to any outside interference. The Senior Board was the overall governing body.

Each of the boards were independent of each other and there was little co-operation between them. In actual fact, they often took satisfaction in taking shots at each other. There was often conflict concerning venues for matches, clashing of fixtures, non-appearances of referees, lots of issues. The boards met each week and they were no more than talking shops, as the fixtures had already been made by the various secretaries. In actual fact, there was no need for weekly meetings.

IT COULD NOT be said that the GAA in Dublin was in a very healthy state. Soccer was the main interest of the sporting public, particularly English soccer and as a consequence interest in gaelic games was very low. Attendance at games was very poor.

The financial situation was not healthy, with a deficit of approximately £70,000, and with little prospect of doing anything about it. After much thought and reflection, I came to the conclusion that drastic steps were required if the situation was to be improved. However, I was well aware that the ultra-democratic system in the GAA would make it difficult to bring about major structural change.

I set up a committee of non-board members, mainly younger people.

Paddy Costello, a colleague of mine in the Sugar Company and the Chief Work Study Officer joined the committee as well. It was a brilliant committee and they were not hindered by any of the past practices or structures. They took a full year to come up with a report.

They studied the situation under the following heading:

1. Structures
2. Administration
3. Finances
4. Development

They came up with the following proposals which were, in GAA terms, revolutionary to say the least.

1. General management to be by 'committee' rather than by 'board' system.
2. Appointment of full-time administrators.
3. Dublin should get 5% of all gate receipts at Croke Park, plus the cost of the full-time officers.

Obviously, these proposals were dramatic.

They had to be voted on and accepted at county convention. It took a second meeting and after much debate and opposition the new system was accepted. This taught me a salutary lesson that the silent majority should be listened to more often. The main opposition came from the same few conservatives who too often got their way. I was delighted with myself for having the courage to challenge the status quo.

The new proposals had now to go to Leinster Council and Central Council before we could put the wheels in motion. While there was opposition from some counties, there was agreement on two points. Both councils agreed to contribute €2,000 each for the cost of two full-time officers… and Dublin would get 2.5% of all gates at Croke Park.

The following committees were set up:

1. Management Committee: to deal with the general running of the GAA in Dublin, including finance and day-to-day activities.
2. Activities Committee: to deal with competitions, fixtures.
3. Grounds Committee: to deal with allocation of pitches.
4. Referees Committee: to deal with the appointment of referees.
5. Disciplinary Committee: to deal with player indiscipline.

The two full-time officers appointed were Jim King, who in effect became the CEO, and Donal Hickey, who became Development Officer. Actually, the Central Council only gave permission for one official, but I took it upon myself to make two appointments which drew a certain amount of ire from Croke Park. I saw both positions as vital if we were to achieve the aims set out in the committee report.

I got one or two letters from Croke Park, asking to explain myself. We were very fortunate at the time to have an excellent president in Pat Fanning. He recognised the importance of the GAA in Dublin to the whole association. I had to pay a visit to Croke Park to meet the president and Seán Ó Síocháin, the Ard Stiúrthóir.

During a very amicable meeting, Pat said to me, 'You know Jimmy, there was only one full-time officer agreed!'

'Yes I know that,' I responded. 'But it is crucial that the area of development is covered, which came out very strongly in the report. So I took a chance that it wouldn't be noticed by you people.'

Pat replied, 'Well Jimmy, fair dos to you… I probably would have done the same myself. We will leave it at that, and I will push it through!'

This whole process took about two years. They say it is easier to get forgiveness than permission. I get a lot of praise for the appointment of Kevin Heffernan as Dublin manager in 1973 but I feel my biggest contribution to the GAA has been the total reorganisation of the Dublin County Board I helped bring about.

Paula Lee was full-time secretary. Mick Leahy was a part-time assistant secretary. He was a great servant of Dublin GAA. The board expanded rather quickly as more and more work had to be done. Jim King asked John Costello to come in as an assistant on a voluntary basis. But Jim told me his plan was that John would replace himself, when he stepped down.

John was the representative of the Erin's Isle club. I encouraged John to apply for the full-time job when it came up. It was an inspired decision, as John has turned out to be a marvellous executive. He is responsible for a lot of the developments in Parnell Park.

I ALWAYS FELT that the real strength of the GAA would be in strong and stable clubs in the city and county. This would be the main responsibility of Donal Hickey, the Development Officer. Donal and myself sat down and drafted a plan which would be a blueprint for development in the future.

We defined a strong and stable club as one linked to a particular area and having a clubhouse that would guarantee permanence. We would also need to establish new clubs in some areas and promote amalgamation in other areas. Looking back now, the amalgamations have worked well. For example, Crumlin GAA club is an amalgamation of St Columba's and St Agnes' while... St Ciarán and Craobh Rua came together and is now Craobh Chiaráin.

Putting the plan down on paper was the easy part but putting it into practice was not as easy. The northside of Dublin was pretty well provided with good clubs. The number of clubs in the south, however, was thin on the ground. The city was expanding at a rapid rate, especially north-west and south-west of the county. Tallaght was a prime example.

It is fair to say that gaelic games were not very popular in Dublin in the 60s and early-70s and, in actual fact, there was an apathy in Dublin in this respect. English soccer had a very big following at that time. The B&I boat was usually packed with supporters going to Liverpool and Manchester, departing on Friday night and returning on Saturday night. This was the climate that prevailed at this time, so the job of implementing our development plan was a major challenge.

Despite the best efforts of Donal Hickey, and many more enthusiasts, progress was very slow indeed.

Then 'The Dubs' arrived on the scene!

After they won their first All-Ireland in 1974, the whole atmosphere in Dublin changed. Interest and support was huge and new clubs sprung up all over the county and, as a result of this massive growth, the GAA is now the most popular sporting body in Dublin. The GAA will be forever indebted to Kevin Heffernan and his players for the revolution they started.

HOW THE DUBS of the 70s came about is a different story.

It has been told so many times how I got Kevin Heffernan to take the job of managing the team. Suffice to say that not all stories are quite accurate.

I always believed that a successful inter-county team was vital for the promotion of the game in the county. This was particularly true of a county like Dublin where competition from other sports, especially soccer, was intense. In the late-60s and early-70s Dublin football was at a very low ebb with regular early exits from the championships in hurling and football. Football was more popular than hurling and while my own preference would be for hurling, I felt that to be more realistic about it, more concentration needed to be given to football.

I made up my mind that it was time to change the selection system. The selection committee at the time was composed of two members from the county champions and three members from the county committee. Apart from being unwieldy, particularly on match days, there nearly had to be committee meetings on match days to make changes. This is a slight exaggeration, but not totally untrue.

My first experience of the system was when I was told by Jim King that I was an ex-officio member of the selection committee and that I should attend. I found it hard to understand why I should be present even though I would have no say when it came to picking the team. When I attended the first meeting, I was amazed at how the process worked.

There was little or no thought given to the practical or tactical aspects of selection. I made my mind up that it was time to make changes. I felt that a fair amount of time should be given to all aspects of team selection, players for various positions and a team plan for the day. This did not happen.

I knew Kevin Heffernan for over 40 years and we often discussed the game and how it should be played. He was a highly intelligent person in every way, including his knowledge of football. He thought seriously about it and how it should be played. He had a marvellous capacity to identify players for the various positions on the pitch.

I decided that the team management would be comprised of three people that I would pick. I needed the sanction from the County Committee, which

I got. Jim King told me that I hadn't a chance in hell of getting it through the committee. In actual fact, it went through with very little objection.

I had planned Kevin as manager, with Lorcan Redmond and Donal Colfer as selectors. Denis Skehan recommended Donal Colfer to me. It was probably the best decision I ever made. However, it was not all plain-sailing... as Kevin at first refused.

He had promised his own club St Vincent's that he would take over the running of the senior football team. I pleaded with him to reconsider. Kevin was a great clubman and I fully understood his predicament.

The great Seán Óg Ó Ceallacháin arrived on the scene and unwittingly played a major part in getting Kevin to change his mind. Seán Óg was the GAA correspondent of the *Evening Press*. He rang me one day and enquired how progress was going with the appointment of a new management team?

I told him that I was doing everything possible to get Kevin Heffernan to take over. The following Wednesday's Evening Press headline was that Kevin Heffernan was to take over the Dublin job as manager. The following morning, Kevin rang me and his exact words were... 'Where did they get you from?'

I said I had nothing to do with it but that I was thankful to Seán Óg. I won't quote what Kevin said next but he added, 'I suppose I can't back down now! Anyway thanks... I appreciate being asked!'

What followed were years of great success, some failure, but a great time in which the GAA in Dublin was reborn and it continues to this very day. Thanks to three wonderful mentors and a bunch of footballers.

The GAA in Dublin is now in a very strong place. We have strong clubs in nearly all parts of the city and county. They are working really hard promoting gaelic games in their own areas. The nurseries have been a great success over the last 10 years. We have a very efficient and effective County Board and a CEO, who I hope will be in the job for many more years. It fills me with pride that I have made a contribution to this very satisfactory position in the life of Dublin GAA.

There is often conflict between club and county in all counties. Both units are equally important. The club promotes the games at local level, and a successful county team sells the games to young people.

It is worth noting that the County Board had a deficit of £70,000 in 1969 and this was cleared in '74, the year the Dubs won their first All-Ireland of that era.

I AM VERY proud of the fact that I was made president of Dublin GAA. The Dublin project is one to be very proud of and I am just delighted to have been a very small part of it. The evolution of the board has been fairly painless, going from one administration to another.

I list here the former chairmen and secretaries of Dublin GAA.

They made Dublin what it is today.

◄◄◆▷▶

DUBLIN COUNTY BOARD
CHAIRMEN 1886 – 2021

John Wyse Power	No club	1886 – 1888
Joseph Bolger	'98 Club	1888
Tom Lee	Erin's Pride	1889 – 1891
Jim Boland	PW Nally's	1892
JJ Kenny	Erin's Hope	1893
M Brady	Raparees	1894
Pat Tobin	Brian Boru	1895 -1896
JJ McCabe	Commercials	1897 – 1898
Frank Burke	Hibernians	1899
Pat Cullen	Faughs	1899
Tony McGeogh	Hugh O'Neill's	1900 – 1901
Hugh McCarthy	Avon Rovers	1902 – 1903
Tony McGeogh	Hugh O'Neill's	1904 – 1908
JJ Hogan	Davis HC	1909 – 1911
Harry Boland	Faughs	1911 – 1918
Andy Harty	Faughs	1918 – 1925
Pat Kennefick	Young Ireland	1925
Seán Ryan	UCD	1926 – 1928
Jim 'Builder' Walsh	Faughs	1928 – 1930
Tom Brown	Round Towers Clon	1930
Seán O'Connor	Geraldines	1930 – 1932
Major Tom McGrath	Army Metro	1932 – 1934

Paddy McDonnell	O'Toole's	1934 – 1939
Seán Ó Braonáin	Civil Service	1939 – 1948
Tom Russell	St Brigid's	1948 – 1957
Denis Mahony	St Vincent's	1957 – 1960
Tom Loftus	Foxrock Geraldine's	1960 – 1968
Jimmy Gray	Na Fianna	1968 – 1980
Don Cotter	O'Dwyer's	1980 – 1986
Phil Markey	St Sylvester's	1986 – 1990
Con Clarke	O'Tooles	1990 – 1993
John Bailey	Cuala	1993 – 1998
John Egan	Clanna Gael/Fontenoy	1998 – 2000
John Bailey	Cuala	2000 – 2006
Gerry Harrington	Naomh Mearnóg	2006 – 2010
Andy Kettle	Fingal Ravens	2011 – 2014
Seán Shanley	Craobh Chiaráin	2015 – 2019
Mick Seaver	Erin's Isle	2020 –

SECRETARIES – HONORARY AND PERMANENT 1915 – 2021

Lorcan O'Toole	Hon		1915 – 1940
Robert Freeman	Hon	Westerns	1940 – 1945
Harry Conlon	Per	Geraldine's	1945 – 1949
Robert Freeman	Hon	Westerns	1949 – 1957
Ted Cooling	Hon	Clanna Gael	1957 – 1965
Jim King	Hon	O'Connell Boys	1965 – 1970
Jim King	Per	O'Connell Boys	1970 – 1995
John Costello	Per	Erin's Isle	1995 –

DUBLIN COUNTY BOARD MEETING PLACES

1895	4 Gardiner St
1887 – 1888	42 Upper O'Connell St

1889 – 1902	27 Upper Ormond Quay
1908 – 1916	68 Upper O'Connell St
1917 – 1920	65 Parnell St
1921 – 1923	68 Upper O'Connell St
1923 – 1935	9 Burgh Quay
1935 – 1937	78 Upper O'Connell St
1938 – 1939	9 Burgh Quay
1940 – 1964	14 Parnell Square
1965 – 1979	6 North Great Georges St
1980 – 1982	Amien St North Star Hotel
1983 – 1996	5 Belvedere Place
1996 –	Parnell Park

◄◄◆►►

JOHN COSTELLO

The modern world loves lists – The Top 10, The Most Influential, The Greatest, etc. No matter what criterion you use for such rankings, the name of Jimmy Gray would be towards the summit in terms of his involvement and influence on gaelic games in the capital.

If there was a virtual Mount Rushmore in the county the figure of Jimmy Gray would be etched there.

A former senior footballer and hurler, Jimmy played in goals on the last Dublin team to reach an All-Ireland Senior Hurling Championship final Sunday… back in 1961.

People like Jimmy have put their shoulder to the wheel ever since, in whatever way they could, to try to get Dublin back to such exalted levels. Following his playing days, Jimmy was also an outstanding administrator at Dublin and provincial level where his vision and acumen was outstanding.

He was central to the appointment of Kevin Heffernan as our senior football manager back in the early 1970s – the success of the team of that era breathed new life into gaelic football at both a local and national level. A time when it was really needed.

Many new clubs emerged in Dublin around this era, as the desire to play our national games spiked. The heroes of the 70s will be spoken about whenever and wherever gaelic football is discussed… 'heroes of renown' for certain.

As far back as 1970, Jimmy presented a document to the Dublin County Board outlining his blueprint and vision of the future. To reflect on some of it now is most enlightening – the document presents a clear, determined picture of a pathway for gaelic games in the capital.

Subjects included in his vision, among others, were club development, upgrading of club facilities, improving facilities from a players' perspective, greater commercial activity, floodlighting Parnell Park, and the importance of a proper and regular programme of games for our juvenile players.

When you read the metaphor, 'Standing on the shoulders of giants' it is when describing Jimmy Gray that this expression is most apt.

On a personal level, Jimmy encouraged me to apply for the role of county secretary and throughout my career he has provided an independent perspective and unbiased advice to me. He has always been a reliable sounding board on current issues and strategy. I will always be grateful for his encouragement, guidance, and support.

JOE ROWLEY

I am not too sure how I first linked up with Jimmy Gray.

Jim King was a great family friend and he would call to our house once or twice a week. He was a member of the Minor Board. I was running the minor team in Scoil Uí Chonaill. In 1960, I was the honorary secretary of Scoil Uí Chonaill and Jimmy was playing senior hurling for Na Fianna and Dublin at that time.

We had two lads on the Dublin senior hurling team – Larry Shannon and Mick Bohan. So it is possible I came in contact with Jimmy through them.

I had a meeting with Jimmy in the College of Science, which is in the Department of the Taoiseach. I recall talking about the management structures in the Dublin County Board. We were discussing Coiste na Réiteoirí. We gave the Coiste power to appoint referees and have their own jurisdiction.

Jimmy has no recollection of that meeting now. My next memory was in 1970 when we had a motion that went to congress. I represented my club and spoke on the motion. We were staying in Ostán Ceathrú Rua out in Connemara. My wife Mary was with me and Jimmy was there with Gretta and the two girls.

One night, Mícheál Mac Liamóir was there with Seamus Ennis. We had a big session and I had my fiddle and that's my claim to fame. Jimmy was one of the driving forces behind Scór when it started in the early-70s. Jimmy set up a committee under the chairmanship of Tom Wolfe. On that committee were Anne Dolan, Donal Hickey, Gerry Davey, Tom Crotty and Martin Bates. Representing our club were Antóin Mac Gabhann and Paddy Glackin. They came first and second in the Scór competition and they subsequently won Fleá Ceol na hÉireann. Students from UCD won the ballad group competition, singing An Bonnán Buí.

Clontarf Golf Club is a haven for Jimmy. He plays golf every Tuesday and Friday, and he is highly competitive. He is loved by everybody in the club. He loves a game of golf, followed by a nice bit of food and a glass of red wine.

He was captain of the Bohemians Golf Society. The society would visit various golf clubs for their outings and then they would put on a show that night.

He was also involved in the 2K Investment Club. We were a group of friends who would meet socially and invest a few bob here and there. We actually did well out of it even though the main function was social.

The story goes that the criteria for a job in the Sugar Company had nothing to do with your ability, but more with your hurling prowess. This young hurler applied for a job and the interviewer asked him a few easy questions and he didn't do too well. So his final question was, 'Would you agree that Carlow is about 50 miles from Dublin?'

He answered, 'Yes' and got the job.

When we travel to matches now, Jimmy is known by everybody and they want to chat. Jimmy is a massive Na Fianna man.

We followed Cuala when they won two All-Ireland club finals. One day, I said to him, 'Jimmy, I can't believe you are shouting for another Dublin club.'

He loves his hurling, especially Dublin hurling.

He is a wonderful man and a great friend.

◄◄◆►►

Jimmy was instrumental in appointing Kevin Heffernan as Dublin football manager in 1973 and quickly saw The Dubs back on top of the GAA world. Jimmy and Gretta with the Sam Maguire Cup (above) after Dublin defeated Galway in the 1974 All-Ireland final and (left) his own kids were not shy in also showing their affection for the Boys in Blue.

« CHAPTER 7 »

The Ban

I WOULDN'T BE an expert on the famous Rule 27... The Ban.

But I certainly didn't agree with it. I saw it as an impediment to the promotion of gaelic games, particularly in Dublin where we have lots of different groups of people who like to do their own thing.

I don't think banning 'foreign games' does anything to promote Irish culture.

I never saw one benefit from banning the playing or attendance at soccer or rugby games.

I don't recollect many suspensions in Dublin, either.

One that stands out, however, was Con Martin, who played soccer for Ireland and Aston Villa and Drumcondra. Con was a very decent man, who won a Leinster medal with Dublin in 1941. He played gaelic football with the Aer Corps and he was an excellent centrefield player.

Anyway, when they were giving out the medals for the Leinster final Con didn't get one because of his soccer activities. As a consequence, he missed out on the 1942 All-Ireland final. I knew Con very well and he was a regular visitor to Croke Park, and he really loved gaelic football.

I imagine one of the reasons he played soccer was to supplement his income, as the Aer Corp wages wouldn't have been wonderful at that time. I played a lot of golf with Con... he was an excellent golfer as well. He wasn't a great soccer fan and I think he didn't hold the FAI in the highest regard.

Another case was Paddy Neville, who played for Parnells. He also played in goal for Drumcondra… so he got suspended too.

WASN'T IT IRONIC that the decision to delete rule 27 happened in Queen's University Belfast? The Troubles were getting worse and worse, and internment was introduced in August of 1971. Rule 28 included vigilance committees.

Members of this committee could attend soccer, rugby and hockey matches to catch GAA players. Breandán Ó hEithir put it beautifully when he said the function of a vigilance committee member was to spot… 'The straying sheep among the graceless goats'. Rule 29 was about attendance at non-Irish dances.

Shortly before congress, there was a major row in Belfast over the venue for the McRory Cup semi-final. Two Belfast catholic schools, St Mary's and St Malachy's were drawn to play each other. St Malachy's were the holders and St Mary's had a real good team, so it promised to be a game not to be missed.

On the St Malachy's team was Martin O'Neill from Derry, who was an outstanding footballer. He was also a top class soccer player… he played for Distillery in the Irish league. The ban didn't apply to schools or college competitions, still members of the Antrim Board felt that the game should not be played in Casement Park because of O'Neill's soccer involvement.

So, you had the farcical situation of two Belfast schools having to travel to Omagh to play the semi-final. It left a poor taste in a lot of people's mouths. Incidentally, St Mary's won and they went on to win the Hogan Cup.

TOM WOLFE, A Kerryman and a member of the Civil Service Club, led the battle to get rid of the ban and the more I heard him talking, the more I agreed with him. Tom was a very intelligent man and had a very persuasive argument for its removal.

He had lots of facts and figures to back up his argument.

He used to remind us that Dr Croke was totally against the ban. He went on a bit too long at the annual conventions and he turned off some people, but he was correct in all he said about the stupidity of the ban. Eventually, it was agreed that Tom could only raise the ban issue at every third convention.

Tom was a founder of the Civil Service Club and he did wonderful work in the early days, and was very much involved when the land in Islandbridge was purchased. He was also chairman of the Scór committee in Dublin.

Con Murphy from Cork rang me one day looking for Tom's number, as he felt aggrieved by something Tom said in an interview. 'I searched the phone directory, but I couldn't find his name?' said Con.

I told Con that Tom was in the directory as Tomás de Bhuilf. Con was stunned as he felt Tom was a bit of a 'West Brit'.

He was a fluent Irish speaker as well.

THE BAN NEVER had huge support in Ireland. A few very influential people like Alf Murray and Pat Fanning, two excellent and sincere men, were very pro-ban and when they spoke, a lot of people just shut up. Dublin normally brought a motion to congress to remove the ban and when those influential people spoke, that was the end of the matter.

Normally, it would pass the Dublin convention with a big majority. There were a few pro-ban people and they would be listened to as they were very sincere. One year, Seamus O Nualláin, a pro-banner, was absent from our county convention and when he was told that Dublin was bringing the motion to Congress, he commented, 'Don't worry, congress won't pass it'.

PADDY MCDONNELL, A member of the O'Toole's Club, and his brother Johnny, were great players in their day and they won two All-Irelands with Dublin in the 20s. Both of them were in the Jacob's Garrison in 1916, and they joined Michael Collins in the War of Independence. Paddy was a very strong ban man, and he and I had many arguments on the issue.

I asked him one day were there many soccer players in the GPO? He confirmed to me that there were a good few soccer lads there. Jimmy Wren, author of *The GPO Garrison, Easter Week 1916* confirmed that a lot of soccer players were in the various garrisons during Easter Week.

The vigilance system was, in my opinion, a form of spying, and surely to God our history should have taught us that informers brought down nearly every movement in Ireland. All of the Dublin chairmen were very broad-minded and hadn't much time for the ban. They were strong GAA people and their main function was to actively promote gaelic games. I know in other counties, however, the vigilantes were very active.

In Limerick, for example, it was well known that Mick Mackey loved going to 'foreign games.' So as to avoid the embarrassment of having to suspend him, they put him on the committee and therefore he could attend any games he wished.

Jack Boothman, the former GAA president, was invited to join the Wicklow vigilance committee but he declined when he was told that the members' names would not be in the public arena. He is reported as saying, 'I will not be a member of any secret society'.

I LOVED TO see a good rugby game and went to a good few during those days. My friend Brendan and I decided to go to Lansdowne Road to see Ireland play England. Brendan was our club secretary and a member of the Dublin senior football squad.

As we were approaching Lansdowne Road, who did we see across the street from us but Tom Loftus, the Dublin chairman. When Brendan saw him he said to me, 'We're done, we're in big trouble now. There will be a board meeting... we will be named.'

I wasn't sure that Tom saw us.

Anyway, we went to the game, but Brendan was getting more worried by the minute. Just to appease him, I told him I would phone Tom the following day to see how things were. Tom worked in the ESB, and he was a great friend of Kevin Heffernan.

I rang Tom and, after the usual chat, I asked him was he aware that Brendan and myself were at a rugby game in Landsdowne? 'Ah, don't be worried about that, I was there myself and when you saw me I was waiting for my son... we really enjoyed the game.'

In 1968, Manchester United played Shamrock Rovers in the first round of the European Cup in Dalymount Park. Kevin Heffernan, Paddy Donnelly and I were going to the match to see the Busby Babes. We were walking along Phibsborough Road and there was Mr O'Neill, a member of Na Fianna and a pro-banner, and we were afraid that he might report us.

He came over and said to us, 'I hope ye are not going to the soccer match!'

'No... No!' we said, 'We're going to the Bohemian Cinema.'

He walked behind us, so we had to pay into the cinema... and then come out a few minutes later and go to the match.

AT ONE STAGE Croke Park set up a committee to decide the justification for the retention of the ban. This was a result of a congress meeting, when the vote to retain the ban was slim enough.

I was invited to attend a meeting and I told them that I was very much in favour of getting rid of the ban, and I said that if you stood outside Dalymount Park or Lansdowne Road at an international match you could suspend over half the inter-county hurlers and footballers.

I played a bit of soccer for a local team called Haroldfield.

We were a very small club made up of local lads from Drumcondra. I recall on one occasion I was ready to play a game for the club and I looked over at the side of the field, and I noticed this avid ban-man... so I slipped away and didn't play at all. The ban also included attendance at 'foreign dances'.

Rugby clubs were making good money running dances at weekends. It was very hard to raise money in those days, and dances and raffles were the best events to get some money. One rugby club had a dance every Saturday night in one of the CYMS halls and they were cleaning up. We, in Na Fianna, needed money to get things done.

Tom Fitzpatrick suggested that we run dances, but there were objections saying we can't do that because of the ban. Mossy Fitzgerald, a Kerryman and a brother-in-law of mine, was a great fundraiser for the club. He suggested that we meet in the Rainbow Café on O'Connell Street to discuss tactics.

We met at 7pm one evening, and it was decided that we could describe ourselves as a philanthropic society and thereby could run dances tax free. Mossy had all details worked out and the only remaining snag was that we couldn't go under the name of Na Fianna.

We discussed a lot of other names but we were finding it difficult to agree on one. So Mossy said, 'We are here in the Rainbow Café... let's call ourselves the Rainbow Club'. For years afterwards, we ran dances under our new name.

We moved around to different clubs like The Crystal, The National and The Country Club. We made serious money which went to Na Fianna and it was a great help to promoting our projects. In the National Ballroom we couldn't jive and if you tried it you were put out. We couldn't afford the top show bands.

One of our committee had a contact with one of the lads in the Clipper Carlton and we were delighted to go with that, as we knew they would attract a very big crowd. But we had to discuss a suitable venue, and we felt the Mansion House would be the best. It fell apart when we were told that the band would need one third of the receipts. So we pulled the plug on that one immediately.

Billy Watson and his orchestra always attracted big numbers. It wasn't a real orchestra but they were dressed in bow-ties and looked the part. We used to go to monthly dances in Shandon Tennis Club and a priest would drop in every night and look around to make sure we were all conducting ourselves. The church was very powerful then.

I was Dublin chairman when congress was held in Belfast in 1971. In the months leading up to congress, county conventions voted to get rid of the ban and plebiscites were held and the result was very much in favour of throwing it out.

As far as I can recall, only two counties voted for its retention – Sligo and Antrim. Pat Fanning was the Uachtarán and he was very much a pro-ban man. But he respected the wishes of the majority of the members of the GAA and to his eternal credit, he suggested that the motion should be passed without taking a vote on it. Armagh proposed the motion, and I asked Tom Wolfe to second it.

Tom was chuffed to be asked, but I felt he had worked so hard for this day and he deserved his moment in the sun. Not only did Tom raise the issue at Dublin conventions but he frequently appeared in the letters to the editor in *The Sunday Independent*. So he was well known nationwide. He was a wonderful man.

One of the many good memories of that weekend was a sing-song we had one night – the Fear an Tí invited every county to make a contribution. When he called on Cork, nobody came forward. So he said he would come back again later.

Still Cork had no volunteer. So Con Clarke, one of the Dublin delegation got up and sang, *The Banks of my own lovely Lee*. He got a wonderful ovation. Con was a lovely singer. He became Dublin chairman in due time and made a great contribution at club and county level. He hails from the O'Toole's club.

◂◂◆▸▸

BRIAN DUNCAN
(Clanna Gael player and a member of Friends of Dublin Hurling)

The ban never really applied in Dublin. I won an under-21 Football Championship with Clanna Gael where the outstanding player for us was John O'Shea, subsequently of Goal fame, who was playing senior club rugby at the time.

A few years later, I was a 'mentor' with a Clanna Gael under-21 football team which lost the championship final due to a mighty performance by Eoin Hand of Scoil Ui Conaill who scored freely from frees and '50s'. Everyone in Dublin GAA knew Eoin was playing professional soccer in England at the time.

To their credit the club decided not to lodge an appeal.

Mick Lynch, who was playing soccer with Shamrock Rovers, played many a game with Clans seniors.

I even played a junior hurling match with Dick Spring, former Tánaiste and Labour Party leader. I met him again recently and he fondly remembers the occasion.

While not related to the ban one of the most interesting 'cross overs' is Mick Byrne, who after winning senior football and junior hurling championships in the same year with Clanna Gael, became famous as the physio on the wonderful Jack Charlton Irish team.

One final ban related memory. Organised by Chris Kane through his Bord Failte contacts, Clans made a visit to Glasgow in the 1970s. Ted Cooling, who at the time was secretary of the Dublin County Board, was on the trip and was persuaded to go to a match in Ibrox Park (Celtic were playing away that week). It was probably just as well social media wasn't around at the time.

CON CLARKE
(Dublin Chairman 1990–'93 and delegate to 1971 Congress)

We stayed in the Europa Hotel and there was a big security paling around the perimeter. Every morning a unionist brass band would parade outside the hotel.

We had a delegation of 12. We went on a bus tour and we saw the troops and tanks on the road. We got stopped a couple of times, but everybody seemed to laugh it off. Once you got back into the hotel, you stayed there. It was said that some delegates got confession before travelling to Belfast. But, thankfully, nothing untoward happened and we had a good congress.

Tom Wolfe made the presentation and Don Cotter, Jimmy Gray and myself spoke. Only two counties voted to retain the ban. I was delighted that Cork weren't one of the two because if Frank Murphy wasn't on your side, you were doomed. He was a very convincing speaker and highly respected.

One year, at another congress, we had a motion in favour of changing the sponsorship rule. I remember Fr Leo Morahan from Mayo standing up and saying, 'Let me address the men from the Pale'. We were happy with our presentation and we felt we had the vote to carry the motion.

We had two delegates from Mayo sitting beside us and we knew they were on our side. But just before the vote was called, they got up and walked out. We begged them to wait but they were gone. We just about got the vote through and, afterwards, we bumped into the two Mayo lads who had walked out.

We asked them why they left and they told us that they were from Fr Leo's parish and if they had voted in favour of the motion, he would proscribe them from the altar. So, they told him they were short taken and had to go out as they felt the best thing to do was not to vote at all.

We had a vigilance committee.

They were appointed at county committee level and not at convention, so very few people knew who they were. Ted Cooling headed it up for a long time. I used to play a bit of hockey if I had no football or hurling. A good friend of mine, Jack Thompson, used to run the Railway Union third team and he would call me if they were stuck.

I went out to Skerries one day to play for my friend and when I arrived into the pavilion who was inside, but Ted Cooling. I never knew that Ted played hockey. So I came out and said to Jack, 'I can't tog out because there is a fella in there from the county board and he will have me proscribed'.

'Don't worry!' says Jack, 'he is playing himself'.

I couldn't believe it. So I went back into the pavilion and poked Ted in the back and said, 'What are you doing here Ted?' To put it mildly, he was taken aback… and he turned all colours.

◄◄◆►►

Jimmy and some of his best friends, including Kevin Heffernan, risked being banned from the association when going to Dalymount Park to see Manchester United (and George Best, Nobby Stiles and Bobby Charlton) in action. The GAA ban however did hit the former Dublin footballer Con Martin (above) who also starred for Aston Villa and the Republic of Ireland. Martin O'Neill (below) was also shadowed by the ban during his young gaelic football days.

« CHAPTER 8 »

The Heffo Years

I MET KEVIN for the first time when we were on opposite teams in a Dublin under-16 colleges match. He was playing for St Joseph's CBS, Fairview... and I was playing for Coláiste Mhuire. After the game, we got on the 24 bus to Marino.

I was sitting beside him on the bus so, just for the sake of conversation I said, 'Hello' to him. The first thing he did was offer me a cigarette. Our first meeting!

Anytime we met in the ensuing years, we would discuss football and hurling. He was a very intelligent man and an outstanding hurler and footballer. He was Head of Industrial Relations in the ESB. I got to know and like his ideas on football. So when I became Dublin chairman I felt Kevin would make a massive difference if I could get him involved. Donal Colfer was equally proficient in his knowledge of football, and Lorcan Redmond knew every footballer in Dublin. So the three of them were a fair team.

When Kevin agreed to get involved he left no stone unturned to get the team up to the top level. He got a training programme from Mickey Whelan, who would become a wonderful teacher, but who was studying for his Masters in the US at the time. Mickey was also a great footballer himself, a former All-Ireland winner with Kevin in 1963, and a future member of the St Vincent's club.

The programme had lots of exercises and drills that were new to everybody, but the players accepted them with relish. Some of the exercises were very physical and a spectator on the bank one night suggested that Heffo was preparing the players for karate, not football. They trained on Tuesday and Thursday evenings, and Saturday morning.

The Saturday morning session caused some consternation but, nevertheless, it continued even on the day before a big game. The players bought into Kevin's philosophy and decided to give it their best shot. Kevin was very good at looking after the players' welfare. Injured players were sent to Kevin O'Flanagan, who was highly rated in this area.

The facilities in Parnell Park were not great, however.

The building was cast iron with a few leaks here and there. We made a few bob in the National League later on, and I said to Kevin that we should build new dressing-rooms in Parnell Park and his response was... 'You will not... we got two All-Irelands out of the ones that are there, and we may get a third one yet!'

He was afraid that the players might get too soft if the facilities were upgraded. After training, the only food the players got was a bottle of milk and a few biscuits. Imagine if a manager today suggested that for his team.

He was a great judge of a player and he knew the type of player he needed for each position.

Another change we made was the introduction of the dark blue knicks. We used to have white knicks, but Mick Dunne suggested that the contrast between the jerseys and the white knicks was not good for television. Paula Lee, who worked in Parnell Park, suggested dark blue as a suitable colour and we took it on board.

Other Dublin agencies have adopted that colour scheme now as well. Down did a similar operation when they changed their knicks to black. There was a bit of consternation in Dublin when we changed as we hadn't informed the executive of the board. They were not one bit happy that they hadn't been consulted. But they got over it.

Of course, when you are winning it is much easier to make such a change. I know a few cases where colours were changed and when the team lost the following weekend, all hell broke loose and certain members blamed the change of colours for losing the game.

We travelled by limos supplied by Jennings... the undertakers.

They cost a fortune – actually two shillings and six pence a mile... and we had five limos. So to save money we decided to travel by bus.

Joe O'Hara of Jennings was not impressed but we had to do it really. While we would have five full limos on the way to a game, only two or three would be used on the way home as some players would travel home with family or friends. There were some objections to the new travel arrangements even though the board saved a lot of money. We went ahead anyway and as I said earlier, when you are winning it is easier to get forgiveness.

Heffo was a man of few words and wouldn't reveal too much to anybody. He loved his cigarettes and whether in the Vincent's clubhouse or Clontarf Golf Club you would frequently see him on his own, reading *The Irish Times* and smoking his cigarette. He was a very good golfer and was club president at one stage.

Actually, he was a wonderful hurler as well and won many senior medals with his club. He was captain of the Dublin football team in 1958 and when they qualified for the All-Ireland final, Kevin and Snitchy Ferguson took a break from the hurling so as to totally focus on the football. Snitchy came back to the hurling, whereas Kevin did not.

Dublin had a poor start to the 70s, losing to Longford in 1970, then losing to Laois in '71. The following year we lost to Kildare and, in 1973 we lost to Louth. In those losing four years Dublin didn't have one All Star winner.

◄ ◄ ◆ ► ►

THE 70s

17 May 1970	Dublin 3-8	Longford 2-14
6 June 1971	Dublin 0-13	Laois 3-8
2 July 1972	Dublin 3-5	Kildare 0-16
10 June 1973	Dublin 0-9	Louth 1-8
22 Sept 1974	Dublin 0-14	Galway 1-6 (All-Irl final)
26 Sept 1975	Kerry 2-12	Dublin 0-11 (All-Irl final)
26 Sept 1976	Dublin 3-8	Kerry 0-10 (All-Irl final)
25 Sept 1977	Dublin 5-12	Armagh 3-6 (All-Irl final)
24 Sept 1978	Kerry 5-11	Dublin 0-9 (All-Irl final)
6 Sept 1979	Kerry 3-13	Dublin 1-8 (All-Irl final)

◄ ◄ ◆ ► ►

THE THREE NEW selectors were given a three-year term when they were appointed in early September 1973. Heffernan was also appointed as coach. A few weeks after their appointment they got a rude awakening when Dublin lost to Roscommon and were relegated to Division 2 of the NFL.

Heffo's credo was to get a group of players and work on their skill, achieve maximum fitness and develop suitable tactics for each game. They lost the Division 2 NFL final to Kildare. Their first championship win was against Wexford.

This game was a curtain-raiser to the Roscommon v Kerry Division One League final. An interesting spectator that day in Croke Park was Jimmy Keaveney. He was a dual player and he had 'retired' in 1972 at the age of 29. There is a story told that a seven-year-old child played a part in getting Keaveney back playing for Dublin. On the journey home after the Wexford game, Kevin was wondering how he could get his forwards to start scoring on a more regular basis.

Kevin's wife's best friend, Lilly Jennings, was in the car with her little boy, Terry. Kevin was thinking out loud when a little voice from the back seat said, 'Jimmy Keaveney never misses frees'. So, Kevin decided to give it a go and the rest is history.

Jimmy accepted the invitation from Heffo to make a comeback and he played in round two of the Leinster Championship against Louth.

◄ ◄ ◆ ► ►

1974 LEINSTER CHAMPIONSHIP

20 May	Dublin 3-9	Wexford 0-06
2 June	Dublin 2-11	Louth 1-9
16 June	Dublin 1-11	Offaly 0-13
14 July	Dublin 1-13	Kildare 1-10
28 July	Dublin 1-14	Meath 1-9

◄ ◄ ◆ ► ►

IT WAS GREAT for Dublin to win Leinster but now we were facing the All-Ireland champions Cork in the semi-final. It was a wonderful game and a great win for us. The crowd went bananas after the game and came on to the pitch to celebrate.

Patsy Devlin from Tyrone was the referee. The following day, the *Evening Press* misquoted me as saying that if Patsy got the final we wouldn't play in it. It was totally untrue and I was very annoyed about it.

When I contacted Tom O'Shea, head of sport in the *Evening Press*, he informed me that a journalist spoke to me on the pitch and he only wrote what I had said. It was a lie, of course. I wrote to Patsy Devlin to inform him that I never said those words. I asked the advice of Tony Hanahoe about demanding an apology, but he recommended letting it go as it would only extend the issue and be a distraction coming up to the final.

There had been wild celebrations on the pitch.

A young Dublin fan, waving a flag, was grabbed by a young garda and Jim King, our secretary, remonstrated with the garda as they were going to arrest him.

GRETTA GRAY

When Dublin reached the All-Ireland final in 1974 Heffo's Army came into being, and the build-up to the big day in Croke Park was something to remember. On their way to Croke Park that Sunday the team met up in Na Fianna's clubhouse on Mobhi Road and we gave them some nourishment in the form of scrambled eggs and tea. Back then, there wasn't the big backroom team as there is today, who would dictate their food intake on the day.

It didn't do them any harm as we all know the result.

◄◄◆►►

WE MET GALWAY in the final, and while they had a lot of good players, they weren't as good as Cork. A major turning-point in the game came when Paddy Cullen saved a penalty from Liam Sammon.

It was a wonderful experience for Dublin to win considering they were in Division 2 in the league and had a very poor championship record in the early-70s. An interesting little story not well known is that Cullen and Sammon were teammates a few months earlier. Cullen had travelled to California as a replacement for Billy Morgan on the All Stars team. Liam Salmon was also on the team.

They practiced penalty shots together in a San Francisco park, with Sammon taking the shots and Cullen in goal.

All of Dublin joined in the celebrations.

There was a parade on the Monday night, starting from St Stephen's Green down Grafton Street, to a platform in front of the GPO. O'Connell Street was packed with celebrating Dublin fans. In the following weeks the cup was brought to clubs and schools all over the county. Paddy Cullen tells a story of visiting a local school with the cup.

The children were assembled in the hall and Paddy was holding up the cup. The principal said to the kids, 'Who is this man holding the cup?'

And one young lad piped up… 'Mr Sam Maguire!'

That win transformed the image of football in Dublin. Young lads had been more interested in playing and watching soccer. The GAA didn't have a good image in Dublin and was fairly disorganised. Games rarely started on time, referees often didn't turn up. Referees had to read the *Evening Herald* to see where they were supposed to be the following Sunday. No wonder some referees failed to turn up.

There was a shortage of referees and some of them were more loyal to the Junior Football and Hurling Boards than to the Senior Board. The various boards were in competition with each other to have first-call on the referees. But that has all changed now and it was wonderful to see what one big win can do to change a whole culture. The new arrangements in Parnell Park ensured that the games were run on a much more professional basis.

FROM 1975 ONWARDS, we had our share of messers on the hill.

They were copying what was happening in England at soccer games. Jim King asked Croke Park to make the final an all-ticket affair so as to in some way reduce the possibility of trouble. Dublin played Derry in a league game around that time and the top of the Cusack Stand was open.

Some of the messers went up to the top of the stand and when the Derry players were going in they started throwing things at them. We were called in to Croke Park to give our response to the trouble. Seán Ó Síocháin reminded us that we were responsible for our supporters and he asked us what we intended doing about it?

I responded saying you can hardly expect the Dublin County Board to control

30,000 supporters. I reminded Seán that I had written to him concerning this issue earlier and I had suggested that a meeting be set up between Croke Park, Dublin County Board and the Gardaí. Seán said that he never got the letter.

I had written the letter from my office... there was an Erin's Food logo on the envelope. His table was covered in paper and when he went out for something, I had a look and there was my letter still unopened. Anyway, that was the end of the matter.

KEVIN MORAN WAS in UCD, and a friend of his, Richie Purcell, the son of Padraig Puirséil, the *Irish Press* journalist, was running the Pegasus soccer team in UCD. They qualified for the FAI Cup.

They had very small numbers and, due to injuries they were struggling to field a team against Dundalk in the cup. Richie asked Kevin would he play and Kevin didn't want to let down his pal, so he agreed. Now Kevin had been picked on the Leinster team to play the same day. Kevin Heffernan and I met him and after he explained his predicament we agreed that he should play for Pegasus.

The Leinster Council were not impressed and Seán Logue from Longford proposed that Kevin be suspended... Billy Lawless from Wicklow seconded the proposal. Now Kevin had written to the Leinster Council explaining his problem and apologising if any offence was taken. Of course, there were no grounds for suspension and to add to that the Railway Cup was on its *uppers* at that stage.

Albert Fallon was Leinster Chairman and the motion was not carried.

A few months later, we played Cavan in a league game in Longford. Kevin had his usual blinder even though he was pulled and dragged all day. Afterwards, when I went into our dressing-room I was taken aback when I saw Seán Logue sitting next to Kevin. I was furious. I asked Kevin why was he chatting to this fellow.

Kevin informed me that this man had asked him to present some medals in Lanesboro and that he had agreed to it, and that Pat O'Neill was going to drive him down. When I told Kevin that this is the guy who wanted him suspended Kevin replied, 'I can't let him down now!' And he did present the medals.

Kevin was a real gent and most obliging.

Kevin was involved in another saga a few years earlier. He had been voted the South City Under-14 footballer of the year. He was playing for St Michael's and James at that time. During the summer the family moved to the Long Mile Road in Walkinstown and bought the Kokonut, a small shop.

The local club, An Caisleán, was delighted when Kevin expressed a wish to transfer to them. The South City league always started in September in those days and there were a few weeks set aside for transfers to take place. All the paper work had been completed and with the agreement of the opposition, Kevin played in a challenge game, even though he wasn't officially a Caisleán player for another week.

His former club were very sad to lose such a player as Kevin and when they heard that he had played before the transfer had gone through, they objected. At a board meeting a few weeks later, they won their case and Kevin was suspended for six months.

During that time he joined a local soccer club just to keep playing and, as they say, the rest is history.

LOSING TO KERRY in the 1975 All-Ireland final really upset Kevin Heffernan, and it caused him many sleepless nights. He knew in his heart and soul that changes had to be made if the younger Kerry team was to be stopped. Heffernan captained Dublin who lost to Kerry in the 1955 All-Ireland final… so he had a *problem* with Kerry.

Dublin's first game in 1976 was a loss to Roscommon in the league.

The forward line at this stage was fairly settled – Anton O'Toole, Tony Hanahoe and David Hickey in the half-forward line, and Bobby Doyle, Jimmy Keaveney and John McCarthy in the full-forward line. In the league semi-final of 1976, Kevin Moran made his debut. In the league final against Derry the half-back line was Brendan Pocock, Pat O'Neill and Kevin Synnott. Kevin Moran partnered Brian Mullins in midfield.

Kevin Moran was settling into a brief role as being one of the greats of Dublin football, a role he had to abandon when he signed for Manchester United. Though he will always remain a *great* in the eyes of all true blue fans.

Dublin went on to win the league final by a point, but the team was now thinking of the possibility of a league-championship double, which last happened in 1958. Dublin had easy wins over Longford and Laois in the Leinster Championship. Meath, in the Leinster final, was a much tighter affair.

We ran out winners by 2-8 to 1-9. Colm O'Rourke, 18 years of age, scored 1-2 but missed a penalty midway through the second-half. The All-Ireland semi-final against Galway was not a great game… the wet conditions and a treacherous pitch played a big part in that. The half-back line was now Tommy Drumm, Kevin Moran and Pat O'Neill. Bernard Brogan was now Brian Mullin's midfield partner. Jimmy Keaveney scored the decisive goal to give Dublin a 1-8 to 0-8 win.

So, now Dublin had a chance to get revenge for the 1975 defeat by Kerry.

Tony Hanahoe told RTE's Mick Dunne in an interview that, 'Dublin played every game to salvage our reputation'. Some journalists reckoned that the burden of history was an issue for the team. Kerry had an unchanged team from the 1975 win and Dublin had newcomers in Drumm and Moran.

Kevin Moran almost scored a sensational goal in the first minute when he ran all the way from centre-back, played a one-two with Bernard Brogan and unleashed a rasper that shaved the left upright at the Hill16 end. It showed that we were up for it.

The game was a low scoring affair. John McCarthy took a great pass from David Hickey and scored a goal which was the difference at half-time.

Shortly after the start of the second-half McCarthy was fouled in the square and Jimmy Keaveney made no mistake with the penalty… a rocket to the top corner of the net.

Anton O'Toole… the Blue Panther, soloed his way through the Kerry defence and gave a beautiful pass to the on-rushing Brian Mullins and he slipped the ball under Charlie Nelligan. Tony Hanahoe scored the last point to give us a 3-8 to 0-10 win.

It was Dublin's first All-Ireland win over Kerry since 1923. The attendance of 73,588 was a new record for the restructured Croke Park. Heffo's determination to beat Kerry and his wisdom in making the changes necessary had been rewarded.

He was a happy man. His restructuring of the half-back line was crucial and decisive. Paddy Reilly, Alan Larkin and Georgie Wilson struggled against the Kerry half-forward line of Pat Spillane, Ogie Moran and Mickey 'Ned' O'Sullivan. Pat O'Neill, Kevin Moran and Tommy Drumm stepped up to the plate and more than held their own with the three Kerry boys.

A great day for Dublin football and the whole county celebrated.

BEATING KERRY WAS a wonderful surprise.

The week before the game I thought Heffo was surprisingly quiet. I didn't make anything of it. After the game he said to me, 'That's it now!'

I thought he was referring to the fact that Kerry had been beaten. I went for a week's holiday with the family to England. I got a phone call during the week informing me of the rumour that Kevin had resigned.

I tried to ring, but I couldn't get him.

So when I got back from the holidays, I rang him and asked was the resigning rumour true? There had been a small bit of upset over the use of the VIP room at the post-match function and I thought he might have been a bit hurt over it. He informed me that he was resigning and that he had called a meeting for the Gresham Hotel on the following Monday night to announce it officially.

'Why in the hell are you resigning?' I demanded '... especially now that we won the final and beat Kerry in the process?'

'Jimmy!' he said, 'We have often spoken about this… you know that it has taken an awful lot out of me.' True, I knew he had an obsession about beating Kerry since that loss in 1955. Kevin was a very deep person and didn't share his thoughts with many people.

So we had the meeting at the Gresham as planned and he informed all present that he felt now was the time to make a change and that the players were in a good position now to move the whole thing on. He mentioned again that it had taken a lot out of him. One of the players asked him was there any specific reason he was resigning?

'Ah there is an amalgam of reasons!' he said.

The players were dumbfounded.

'It has taken a lot out of us as well, and we are not resigning!' David Hickey announced.

WE NOW HAD the problem of getting a successor.

The players were a unique bunch of lads. They were very close, and have remained so. They were also great role models for young people and it was sad to see their disappointment at losing Kevin. We knew it wouldn't be easy to get somebody to take over and get the respect that Kevin had. We tossed around a few names, and most of them I felt would not fit the bill. Tony Hanahoe's name came up a few times. He was a marvellous leader on the pitch. The players had a great respect for him. The only problem was that he was a player and in those days a player/manager was unheard of on GAA teams. I mentioned my idea to Jim King and he felt it would not work because of conflict between the two roles.

But we decided to meet Tony in The Royal Dublin Hotel on O'Connell St. We discussed Kevin's shock resignation and the implications of that. Then I offered my opinion.

'Tony, I think the only person who can carry on the good work that Heffo started is yourself.'

I thought he would refuse, but his response was, 'Thanks very much... I will think about it and get back to you!'

It came up at our next management meeting and of course, we had the usual rumours about the reason for Kevin's resignation. They were all false by the way. There followed a lively debate on who should take over. I made the point about the uniqueness of this group and how close they were to each other and that they were very committed as a team. I mentioned Tony's name... again the obvious reaction was... 'That won't work!'

And... 'Player-managers are okay for soccer but not for our game!'

Anyway, at the end of the discussion it was agreed to offer the job to Tony. When I rang him he said, 'Thanks again. I have been speaking to some of the lads and they seem to be very happy with that'.

Tony Hanahoe turned out to be a marvellous manager.

IN HIS FIRST match, in October in the National League, we were not doing well and, as we were going into the dressing-room at half-time, a committee member said to me, 'I told you that wouldn't work!' They came out in the second-half and won the game.

Donal Colfer and Lorcan Redmond stayed on even when Kevin stood down and those two men were wonderful selectors and. They were there when Kevin Heffernan came back to manage the team, and said their goodbyes only when Kevin decided to go, again, after the infamous 1983 All-Ireland win over Galway, and successive losses to Kerry in the finals of 1984 and '85.

A lot of people at the time said to me that Kevin would be back.

Tony led the team to another All-Ireland title in 1977 with an easy win over Armagh, after a great win over Kerry in the semi-final, in a game that is often referred to as one of the best gaelic football games of all time.

AT THE START of 1978, Kevin Heffernan appeared at the first training session and took over as if nothing had happened.

Tony wasn't too pleased, but didn't make an issue of it. The players were a bit confused but, again, they just got on with it. Dublin glided through Leinster, beating Kildare in the final. Down were our opponents in the All-Ireland semi-final and again we won easily. We would like to forget the final against Kerry, when they scored those five goals against us!

Everything went wrong on the day, and then there was Mikey Sheehy's cheeky goal. Paddy Cullen is often blamed for that goal, but Tony Hanahoe made a good point in *Magill* magazine when he said, 'Paddy was out of his goalmouth arguing with the referee. It should be remembered that there were other defenders on the field who might have covered for his distraction.

'One of the ironies of the goal was that it was a Dublin back who handed Sheehy the ball thereby enabling him to take the kick unexpectedly.'

It was a bad day at the office... but that is sport.

IN 1979 WE had a very narrow win over Offaly in the Leinster final.

Jimmy Keaveney got sent-off in the first-half and we had a real problem getting somebody to successfully kick frees. We appealed the sending off.

I rang Paddy Collins, the referee, and I asked him what was he going to report Jimmy for? He said he would wait until after watching *The Sunday Game* before making a decision. The pundits that night agreed that Jimmy was very unlucky to be sent off.

Jimmy never hit anybody.

Ollie Minnock, was the Offaly full-back and he told me that he was not hit by Jimmy. Liz Howard, a pundit on *The Sunday Game*, agreed to come along to the appeal and gave her account of the incident. However, it was to no avail... Jimmy got two months and was ruled out of the All-Ireland final.

We won that Leinster final with a wonderful second-half display. We defeated Roscommon in the All- Ireland semi-final but, again, we lost to Kerry in the final. This time, they scored three goals!

KEVIN'S FINAL ALL-IRELAND win was in 1983, when I was no longer county chairman, and it turned out to be a memorable one. We had to play Meath twice before moving on to the next round, where we had an easy win over Louth. We defeated Offaly in the Leinster final and drew with Cork in the semi-final, and went down to Cork for the replay.

Our supporters travelled in big numbers... what a wonderful weekend! Our lads played really well... we shocked Cork with a big win... and this time we got the goals... four of them!

Galway in the final was a very torrid affair. We ended up, of course, with 12 players on the field... and still won the game. I will always remember Joe McNally being double-marked in the second-half and still getting some critical scores.

Kevin and Lorcan Redmond and Donal Colfer were a wonderful management team. We owed them so much. Heffo laid the foundations for future successes, including the marvellous six in-a-row team in recent times. Jim Gavin continued that tradition of excellent management, and his players were worthy successors to The Dubs of the 70s.

◄ ◄ ◆ ▷ ►

LORCAN REDMOND

My greatest memories of those great years were the actual winning of the All-Ireland finals. The first win against Galway had a massive effect on the whole county and gaelic football became acceptable again in the city.

The other wins weren't as good, as we were half-expected to win them... whereas 1974 was a shock for everybody. Kerry had a very good side and made it very difficult for us.

We won some, and we lost some more.

But they were extraordinary days and we enjoyed all those encounters. There was a great buzz in the city and the county, and we actually had fan clubs all over the country. We changed the style of football and everybody seemed to enjoy it more. Kerry saw what we did and they took it on board, and added to it and beat us at our own game a few times. There was always a special buzz when we met Kerry.

We loved it.

Heffo brought so much to the cause.

You could hear a pin drop when he was talking.

He would often call on one or two players to have an in-put on what happened at the last match, or what we could expect in the next match. The players felt empowered by him and they respected him for that. In the Leinster final against Offaly in 1979 we didn't have a good first-half and, to add to our problems, Jimmy Keaveney had been sent off.

The three of us had a chat at half time out on the sideline.

When we went into the dressing-room Kevin said only a few words. but they had the desired effect and the players couldn't wait to get back on to the pitch. There was no threat to anybody, but the players knew the deal. Our whole game changed in the second-half and we had a great win.

Kevin was a very intelligent man and was able to say harsh words if they were needed... and if a player had to be sorted out then Kevin was the man to do it. Players knew where they stood.

We had the same management team all the time and we got on really well. We all knew what we had to do, and we did it. There were no phone-calls between sessions.

I went to see Kevin Moran playing a club game and I was impressed, and I suggested to Heffo to have a look at him. We invited him on to the panel and we knew early on that he was going to be a great player for us.

Jimmy Gray as chairman was a very astute man.

He was really a hurling man but he gave great support to the team and he was highly respected by all. He had the confidence of Heffo, and that was crucial. Jimmy changed the system of selecting mentors. I was a member of a previous five-man management team and it was too cumbersome. Jimmy introduced the three-man team... and it worked like a dream. As I said we all had our strengths and Kevin oversaw the whole thing.

Yes, it was a wonderful time and I have great memories of those days.

IN THE 70s, it was very common to have requests to play games to fundraise for some charity. Once we hit the headlines in 1974, we got lots of requests and they were all for very good causes but obviously we couldn't agree to them all.

Kerry had similar requests. So we came to an agreement with Kerry that we would play them in Kerry for their charity and, the following year, they would come to Dublin and do likewise. That solved the problem.

The ceiling in the Olympia Theatre in Dublin fell in... thankfully with nobody present. There was a committee set up to raise funds to replace the ceiling. I found myself on the committee and I was requested to check out the possibility of our footballers playing a game in Croke Park to raise some extra cash. I informed the committee that we had an arrangement about fund-raising games and that I would have to go back to the Dublin County Board to get the green light.

The committee, by the way, was a talking-shop and only for Jack Cruise, it would have been hard going. Jack was very funny and I really enjoyed his contribution.

Anyway, permission was given and we got Galway to play us in Croke Park on a Friday night. As a curtain-raiser we had a game between the Jimmy Magee All Stars game and a Dublin team made up of mainly singers, politicians and some sport stars. There was Mark Wilson, Tony Kenny, Johnny Giles, Luke Kelly, Kevin Heffernan and Maureen Potter… just to name a few. I was privileged to be part of the team.

The night was a great success and we made a very sizeable amount of money for the Olympia. We had a presentation of the cheque at a special function. Cecil Sheridan, was the chairman of Equity, and he was there to accept the money from me in the bar at the back of the theatre.

Now Cecil hadn't a clue who I was! He was trying to get the presentation done as he was going somewhere else but he kept spoofing to all and sundry about his 'Very good friend' Jimmy… and how I had arranged the whole fundraiser. Even the press in attendance were getting tired of listening to him, and they asked him to move it on.

Eventually, he called for attention and started his cupla focal.

'I am very glad to accept this cheque on behalf of the committee. I would like to thank my very good friend Mr Jimmy…ahhhh…ahhhh… Jimmy Hill!'

That caused a good laugh from all present. Jimmy Hill was a well-known soccer pundit on the BBC.

Fred O'Donovan was chairman of the Gaiety Theatre and he was on the committee. There was a show in the Gaiety Theatre at the time and there was a group of scantily clad dancers from England taking part. When we were discussing the idea of a programme for the game Jack Cruise said to Fred that he might get the dancers to go on the Hill selling programmes? Fred said it was a good idea, and he would look into it.

Jack was only joking, of course.

All the same, even without the girls on the Hill, we made a nice sum of money and I was glad we did it as we got some very favourable publicity.

We never had a dull moment during those great years in the 70s and 80s.

The Dublin fans loved travelling to away league games and they brought good business to wherever they went. And the Dublin players were delighted to have such a fan base, considering things were so different in the 60s.

Kevin Heffernan's brilliant team management was the reason for all of this. What a wonderful man.

I still miss him every day... and his dry humour.

The Kevin Heffernan era might never have happened if Jimmy Gray did not become Dublin County Board chairman. The glorious 70s has resulted in Heffo (right) being immortalised on Hill 16.

« CHAPTER 9 »

Flying High

THE ALL STAR TRIPS were started by a man called Andy McKenna.

He lived in San Francisco for a while and, when he came back to Ireland, he founded Atlas Travel. He came up with the idea of rewarding the All-Ireland champions and the best footballers and hurlers in the country with a trip abroad.

Our first trip was in 1975 as All-Ireland champions. We went to San Francisco and Los Angeles… a wonderful experience. The players stayed with host families and the hospitality was outstanding.

In 1976, Kerry were champions, so we only had a few players travelling who were part of the All Star team. In 1977, it was our turn again to travel as a full team. However, there was a dispute with the IRA which caused lots of difficulty for all the players travelling.

We had played in the National League final in Croke Park and a group of IRA sympathisers protested on the pitch… and David Hickey, John McCarthy and Paudie O'Shea remonstrated with them.

Their protest was in relation to the treatment of prisoners who were on hunger strike. The Noraid movement in New York created a bit of noise about the Croke Park incident, and John Kerry O'Donnell, the top man in New York GAA, said he couldn't guarantee the safety of the three players

As it transpired, John McCarthy hadn't intended going to America anyway. We decided at board level that unless the full team was going, then we would not travel. Eventually, after a lot of toing and froing we decided to travel after getting confirmation from New York that their ultimatum had been withdrawn.

Our first game was in Chicago.

David Hickey and his brother Michael were the two players now that we were most concerned about. We were taken aback about the amount of security on duty at Gaelic Park. The police had two cars to transport the Hickey brothers.

One car was a decoy. Everything went okay, much to the delight of all concerned and, the same night of that game, Kevin Moran celebrated his 21st birthday. Next, we headed to the West Coast, where once again, everything went really well. We did a lot of sight-seeing during the week. Donal Hickey, Christy Hayes, Gretta and myself drove all the way from San Francisco to Los Angeles on the famous Route 1. The scenery was stunning.

We played the All Stars in a second game in Los Angeles. The night before, we were invited to a reception in a school run by The Franciscans. The priest who ran the school was a brother of our own Fran Whelan.

The lads were having a ball, but a bit of argy-bargy led to a few players ending up in the swimming-pool. Poor old Fr Whelan asked me to get the players to cool it down... he was worried about a heavy fine for such behaviour. The following day, with the temperature in the 90s, we played the All Stars... and we were about 15 points behind by the end of the half.

Brian Mullins gave an incredible display in the second-half and we actually won the game. With a few free days, we drove down to Tijuana, before heading back to New York for the last leg of the trip. Gaelic Park was in poor shape as it had been very wet all that week. Again, nothing untoward happened.

Though, at the very far end of Gaelic Park there were two ladies with a very large banner that read... 'Hooligan Hickey'. We could cope with that.

ANOTHER YEAR, I ended up as manager of the All Stars as Kevin Heffernan couldn't travel. We actually won the series, which I think might have been a first for the All Stars' team. We met a guy called Jim McCluskey out there.

He was from Dublin, but had spent most of his years in San Francisco. He travelled with us everywhere, but we never knew his role. Tony Hanahoe thought he might be from the CIA. Because I was manager, he looked after me and brought me to expensive restaurants... but he never seemed to pay at the end of any of the meals. When we got back to our hotel one night, I noticed Canon Bertie Troy, manager of the Cork hurlers, and Fr Willie Fitzmaurice, a member of the All Stars hurling team, in deep conversation. They seemed a bit agitated.

I asked them had they a problem? They explained that they wanted to say Mass the next morning, but they were told by the archbishop's house that they would have to go to the local church to get permission.

When they contacted the local pastor, he turned them down. My 'new friend', McCluskey, wasn't having this. The archbishop at the time, whose first name was Michael, was away in Rome. McCluskey phoned and asked could he speak to Michael?

He then asked to speak to his assistant and explained the problem that these two Irish priests were having. Again he wasn't having much success.

The best they could do was to give him a number of another neighbouring parish. So Jim phoned that number and spoke to a pastor there, who explained that they had to be… 'very careful in this area… as there are some nutcases around here'.

'Listen!' says McCluskey. 'All these two guys from Ireland need is a goddam place to say a goddam Mass… can you help?'

He eventually agreed and the two priests got a chance to say their Mass the following morning. We found out afterwards that Mr McCluskey was a lobbyist from Sacramento. The CIA had not intervened on the GAA's behalf, which came as some relief.

ON ANOTHER OCCASION, I was in New York on my own.

I was kind of lost and, luckily, I bumped into Eugene Coughlan of Offaly. I regard Eugene as one of the best full-backs of all time. He gave me a guided tour.

We were heading home, and we met Mick O'Dwyer. He invited us to go with him to a restaurant owned by a Kerryman. So, of course, we tagged along and we had a beautiful meal… Mick was full of chat. The owner joined us and we enjoyed his company too.

As it was getting late, we decided it was time to go.

Micko said, 'Hold on until we get the bill!'

It was around $500. Micko handed the bill to me and said, 'There you are, you're a big noise in the GAA… you can pay that!'

I was shocked.

Micko kept a straight face. I was panicking… What am I going to do?

I looked at Gretta.

'Don't worry Jimmy!' he finally said.

'If it's not free… I'll pay for it myself!' he added, beginning to laugh.

Of course, the meal was free… compliments of the owner.

◄ ◁ ◆ ▷ ►

GRETTA GRAY

The Dubs of the 70s were extra special times.

Jim was chairman and he and I had three very memorable trips to America with the All Stars. The first one was in 1975. Not only the teams and officials, but many supporters travelled as well.

When we landed in San Francisco we were met by two pipers, who piped the passengers off the plane. The matches were played in Balboa Stadium, and both Dublin and Kilkenny lost to the All Stars… Dublin by six points.

We hired a car and drove to Los Angeles accompanied by Donal Hickey and the late Christy Hayes. We did the scenic route which was very spectacular. On one part of the coast road it was like hanging onto a mountain on one side, and a sheer drop into the Pacific on the other.

We made a stop in Santa Barbara at a very nice beach where Christy realised his ambition by 'Paddling in the Pacific'.

We went to Los Angeles Airport to meet the team where there were another two pipers and two young girls in Irish dance costumes carrying Irish and American flags. April 1977 was our second trip. We were in the VIP (First Class) section of the plane… luxury. Our first stop this time was in Chicago to be met by three official buses and a police escort to the hotel, while the Hickey Brothers went in a decoy bus… or were we the decoys?

The Hickeys were checked into the hotel under the name O'Malley, and had a police escort for the duration of our stay. Then 1978, was our last All Stars trip. We travelled first-class again. We made a stop in Boston to drop off the hurlers… and then headed on to New York. Jim had seen very little of New York on our previous visit, so this time we took a four and a half hour Grey Line Bus Tour so that he could see the main tourist sights. That night we were at a dinner for the team and were somewhat taken aback when the Toast Master referred to the 'extinguished' guests from Dublin! It nearly was the case, as the last Sunday before we came home there was another game and a farewell dinner. It was enjoyable, even though I was sitting between two priests. But a problem arose after dinner when a crowd of American-born Irish, down from Alaska, who had started a row a few nights earlier, were acting up again in the downstairs bar.

It was agreed that all the Dublin travelling party should slip out the back door when leaving.

Outside, we found four police cars, expecting trouble. We saw so many historic places during our tours. The Golden Gate Bridge, which isn't golden... but painted red. Sausalito where we saw some Giant Redwoods... one was 240 feet high.

The Old Mission Dolores in San Francisco was really something, in particular the churchyard with all the Irish names on the tombstones of people coming from places like Bandon, Limerick, Dublin, Mayo, Roscommon, Meath and Tipperary... who died a few years after coming to America to escape the famine.

One could see the Spanish influence in Monterey and also in San Luis Obispo. In Los Alamos we stopped for petrol and the Sierra Madre Mountains were towering around us. Lots of men were wearing stetsons, but there was no sign of John Wayne. Christy said, 'He's just over the mountains... fighting the Indians'.

A trip to Lake Tahoe, which I would say is the poor man's Las Vegas. We went by coach and climbing steadily, we reached snow-covered hills. When we finally arrived it was bitterly cold. The casino... I thought I had wandered onto a film set – such glitter and glamour, rows and rows of slot machines. Jim tried his hand at these and won $120 dollars (a good amount in those days).

Dublin's runaway success in the 70s meant there was plenty of opportunity to travel to the US on All Star tours, when on one occasion Jimmy had to deputise for Kevin Heffernan as manager. David Hickey (above) was in hot water with IRA sympathisers on one tour, but the travel also allowed friendships to be made (when Jimmy spent time with Kerry rival Mick O'Dwyer).

« CHAPTER 10 »

Looking after Leinster

IN 1967 I was appointed the Dublin delegate to the Leinster Council, and I continued there until I retired as chairperson in '94. I really enjoyed my time meeting delegates from all the other Leinster counties.

Martin O'Neill from Ferns in Co Wexford had been secretary to the council for many years. He had the distinction of refereeing the All-Ireland football final in the Polo Grounds in New York in 1947 between Cavan and Kerry. When Martin stood down, his son Ciarán took over the position.

In due time, Ciarán was promoted to a position in Croke Park and Michael Delaney from Laois became the Leinster secretary. He did a wonderful job and I really enjoyed working with him.

The GAA had produced a commission report where many changes were recommended to help move with the times. When Michael was appointed he was working from home as we had no offices in the province. Obviously, working from home is not really viable when you are getting callers and phone-calls all times of the day and night. During my first year, we decided to purchase an office in Portlaoise. This turned out to be a great success as we could hold all our meetings there. It was also very central for all 12 counties in the province.

THE FIRST MAJOR issue we took on board was to put a structure in place for the organisation and promotion of games in the second level schools in the province. Br Farrell, who had been very involved with second level games for many years, informed me that it was not in a very good place, as games often didn't take place, referees didn't turn up and, sometimes, venues weren't available when two competing schools arrived to play.

I really believed then, and still do now, that our second level schools are vital for the promotion of our games. There were two different bodies running schools games and I thought this was not a good idea. Eventually, after a lot of hard work, we got the two bodies to amalgamate We appointed Michael Reynolds, the current Leinster CEO, as full-time officer to oversee the organisation and running of second level games in the province. He did a wonderful job from the outset. The number of schools participating in competitions grew year-on-year. A lot more games took place, competitions were finished on time and schools really appreciated the new structure under Michael. We were the first province to do this and eventually the other three provinces followed our example.

The next area we tackled was helping clubs upgrade their facilities. This whole area was very ad hoc up to this time and sometimes money could have been better spent. So we appointed a committee, chaired by Jimmy Roche from Wexford, to assist clubs with planning developments. We invited Cathal Mac Mathúna to join this committee.

He was an engineer and his advice in all areas of development was invaluable, and the clubs benefited greatly. We had agreed at council level that any club wishing to embark on developing their playing facilities had to liaise with this committee.

As money was being spent on these projects, we agreed that it had to be spent in the right way. The various counties really appreciated the help from the committee and indeed from the Leinster Council, and a lot of great development took place. It gave me great pleasure to visit some of these clubs when they were officially opening their facilities. Sadly, Jimmy Roche passed away during this period.

We decided to appoint two development officers to help promote our games. Lester Ryan, who sadly passed away only last year, was the South Leinster Development Officer. Colm Brady from Meath was the North Leinster Development Officer.

They did a wonderful job visiting county boards, clubs and schools.

We were inspired by the recommendations from the McNamee Commission Report from Croke Park. It challenged us to really tackle issues that were holding back progress. We knew money would have to be spent, so we put in place people with expertise to bring about change wherever it was needed.

THE REDEVELOPMENT OF Croke Park had an amazing positive effect on all units of the association, and indeed outside the association as well. Croke Park is an incredible project. The chairman of the Dublin Chamber of Commerce asked me to give him a look at the new stadium.

He was astounded when he saw the new Cusack Stand and said that the only other bigger development in North Dublin was Dublin Airport. The feel-good factor inspired county boards and clubs to upgrade their facilities.

Liam Mulvihill and Peter Quinn were centrally involved with this development and the association is deeply indebted to them for their foresight and courage in undertaking such a massive project. Liam's stewardship was very much in evidence during those years. He became Ard Stiúrthóir at a crucial stage of the evolution of GAA. and it was fortuitous that he was there at that time.

I REALLY ENJOYED my three years as chairperson in Leinster. I had to attend lots of meetings, and club and county functions. I met some great characters from the other counties and, generally speaking, we worked well as a team. One of the downsides of big committees is the fact that meetings go on much too long, as certain delegates feel the need to make their point and then to make it again an hour later.

We had a big agenda… discipline, referees reports, finance. We often left Árus Laighean in the early hours of the morning. Things improved slightly when we gave the running of day-to-day issues to the executive. As time went by, the executive assumed more power and their recommendations were generally accepted by the council.

THE COUNCIL'S ONLY source of income was championship gate receipts. Needless to say, every effort was made to keep the top teams apart until the latter stages. Again, in those days, there was no backdoor, just a knock out format.

Lose one game and you were gone for the year.

There was no sponsorship either. So gates were crucial for the proper running of the council. Kilkenny and Wexford were normally kept apart in hurling, as were Dublin and Meath in football. At one meeting, there was a proposal for an open draw in hurling. A lot of discussion followed and much to our surprise it was agreed.

Andy Gallagher, the Offaly delegate, was very much the leader of the move to open up Leinster in hurling. It proved to be a wonderful idea and Offaly appeared in nine Leinster finals in the following decade. A few years later, there was a move to open up the draw for football as well. Again, a lot of discussion took place and eventually it was agreed to have an open draw.

I was in favour of an open draw, as I felt it was a fairer system, especially for the weaker counties. Consternation followed.

What if the top teams are drawn to play each other in round one?

Much to our horror, Dublin drew Meath in the preliminary round of the 1991 Leinster Football Championship.

◄ ◄ ◆ ▷ ►

DUBLIN VS MEATH 1991

		DUBLIN	MEATH	ATTENDANCE
Game 1	June 2	1-12	1-12	51,144
Game 2	June 9	1-11	1-11 (e-t)	60,960
Game 3	June 23	1-14	2-11 (e-t)	63,730
Game 4	July 6	0-15	2-10	61,543

◄ ◄ ◆ ▷ ►

DUBLIN WERE NOT in favour of an open draw, as they normally would play in the Leinster final on the last Sunday in July. I presume Meath were in the same boat.

When the draw was made in November 1990 people were taken aback by the implications of an open draw. The Leinster Council executive feared that their main source of income – a Dublin vs Meath Leinster final – was gone... *and where would the money come from for the various projects they had planned?*

The idea that Dublin or Meath could be out of the championship on June 2 was hard to take.

But it all worked out in the end, much better than the usual seeded draw. Financially, we were in the money as we had four huge gates instead of the usual one. We acknowledged the contribution of the two teams and gave each county €30,000 towards a well- earned holiday.

We gave money to each of the 12 counties in Leinster to promote gaelic games. We also gave a decent sum of money to various charities. We put in place a coaching programme in each county. We made good use of the income we received from the four games.

In the four games Meath had scored a total of 6-44 and Dublin had 3-52, and only one point separated two gallant teams. The total attendance was 237,377.

The gate receipts were £1,055,000.

Both teams were rewarded with their trip to the sun and they well deserved it. So what seemed to be a disaster when the draw was made turned out to be the saviour of Leinster football, and probably nationally as well.

You could say that Jack Charlton's success story at the World Cup in Italy in 1990 was now matched by two great gaelic football teams in '91.

WE ALL HAVE our memories of those fantastic weeks in Croke Park.

As a Dublin supporter, my heart was in my mouth, but as Leinster Council chairman I was rubbing my hands together. We all have moments we can never forget.

Gerry McCaul's term as Dublin team boss had ended in 1990, and Paddy Cullen, our goalkeeper of the 70s, was appointed manager, with Jim Brogan, Pat O'Neill and Fran Ryder his backroom team.

Meath had dominated Dublin in the mid- to late-80s and the Dublin fans were anxious to put a stop to their gallop. In spite of the fact that it was a preliminary round played at the start of the summer, a crowd of over 51,000 turned up for the game, and watched as Dublin had the upperhand. We were leading by 1-7 to 1-2 at half-time. Fans were enjoying the personal duels on the pitch... Colm O'Rourke and Keith Barr, Tommy Dowd and Tommy Carr.

As time was running out, Dublin were leading by only a point. Then came the most agonising moment of the whole day!

Dublin had possession of the ball but David Beggy dispossessed Mick Deegan, who moved the ball on to PJ Gillic. PJ sent a long ball into the square.

John O'Leary came out of his goal and he was keeping an eye on the incoming David Beggy. The ground was extremely hard and the ball bounced over the bar for the equalising point.

I imagine O'Leary often thinks he should have come out a bit more and taken the ball on his chest. Dublin felt they had left the game behind them and Meath felt as if they had won. Myself and my colleagues in the Leinster Council collectively could finally release our breath!

We had another day in the sun for both teams when game two arrived.

THE FANS TURNED out in bigger numbers, just short of 61,000. Barney Rock was back on the Dublin team after his campaigning with the Progressive Democrats in the local elections.

Barney was no spring chicken at this stage but he always *had it* on the big day, and this was a *big day* for both teams. The game was a dour enough contest and at half-time the score was 0-6 to 0-3 in Dublin's favour. Dublin's defence was settled and performing well but there were problems in the forward line and scores were not coming.

Again, we should have won the game. Vinny Murphy had a chance of a point with time running out but he shot for goal... Mickey McQuillan saved it. It was 0-10 each at the end of normal time. We had announced in advance of the game that a draw in game two would mean the necessity to play extra-time. The moment of the day for me?

Two moments in quick succession, actually!

Jack Sheedy scored a goal for Dublin in the extra-time period, but David Beggy stepped up and did the same for Meath quick as you like, almost before we had settled back into our seats. Not that I, as Leinster chairman, could be seen jumping around the place!

Both sides added a point each and, this is still hard to believe... but there was no score for the final 20 minutes.

AGAIN, I FELT drained and sorry for the Dubs, but you had to give it to the Meath boys. They are never defeated... that's one of the many things that Seán Boylan brought to his team.

The crowds was bigger still for game three... June 23 saw 63,730 in Croke

Park. It showed the pulling-power of these two great teams.

Dublin again were the better team, and had a five point lead with only fifteen minutes remaining. Meath scored a fortuitous goal to earn another draw. Gerry Hargan's hand-pass to Paul Bealin was intercepted by Brian Stafford. Colm Coyle ran on to it and passed it on to Bernard Flynn, who finished it off. Another sickener for Dublin.

At this stage most players had given their all and lots of changes were made for the extra-time slot.

On this occasion, it took a late point from Paul Curran to save the day for Dublin. Another day in Croke Park would be needed. The last time it took four games to separate two teams in a Leinster Championship was in 1941, when Wexford played Carlow.

LIKE THE FIRST three games this one was full of incident. Keith Barr clashed with Colm O'Rourke… and Colm came out the worst of it. Dublin were leading by four points and Declan Sheehan was fouled in the square… a penalty! Charlie Redmond was the recognised penalty taker, but he was off the pitch.

It was decided that Keith Barr would take it. He did, but it went wide. Most pundits would say, 'Take your point', especially if you were four points up. Meath battled back and with time running out Vinny Murphy should have sealed it for Dublin.

He hesitated and the ball was won by Meath.

They passed it through so many different pairs of hands, my head was almost spinning… like everyone else in the ground! Finally, a yard from the goal, Kevin Foley slipped the ball underneath the body of John O'Leary. David Beggy added a fast point.

Jack Sheedy had a 60-yard free to equalise. WIDE!

Dublin were shell-shocked. In truth, we all were… and that includes Meath fans!

MORE RECENTLY, I came across an article by John Harrington for *GAA.ie*, written in June 2016, and I think it gives us a great flavour of that epic contest between two great neighbours and rivals. And of the two men on the sideline, who probably had to endure more thrills and heartache than any of us who also watched on.

◄ ◄ ◆ ▷ ►

PADDY CULLEN

The four games, it was wonderful for everyone except our team when they lost. It was hard to take at the time. The expression about 1991 was that you won all four games. But we didn't win one of them. And it felt like that as well… that we had won the four games, when we actually lost. And if you look at it, simple things cost us.

I can't say it was enjoyable. Looking back on it, I don't like looking at the videos, because it is like a movie that you know the ending of. But I am sure in Meath, they re-live it and re-live it and fair play to them, they won it.

What can you do?

We were every bit as good as Meath and better, we just didn't win. People saying it's like a death in the family. It's not. I believe in sport and I believe things can go wrong, things have gone wrong. So what, it's a game.

That's the way I look at it. A lot of people don't like that either, saying it's only a game. They say you're supposed to kill for it. I don't believe in that either. I believe in playing football, I believe in hitting hard and doing your utmost and leaving it on the pitch… whatever you have left in you.

And that's what we did and it worked for the gallery, it worked for the people who came to watch it which was a nice thing too.

SEÁN BOYLAN

We had been beaten in the 1990 All-Ireland final by Cork.

Did we think we were too old? No, but we did think the legs were tired. And that's why we ended up doing all the training in water. Sonia O'Sullivan and Gerry O'Reilly from Dunboyne, who had run in the Olympics as well, were in Atlanta, Georgia and got these buoyancy aids for me for the team. 27 of them cost three and a half thousand pounds.

We had to train in water because their joints were perfect and the ligaments were fine, but their muscles were tired. So training in water re-energised them. We started doing that training in November 1990.

Gerry McEntee had been away and I always remember him coming home and I brought him out to training one night, After we left Gormanston, he said, 'How are you going to face the people of Meath next year when you're beaten in the first-round of Leinster and people ask how training was going… and you have to say ye were f****ng *swimming?!' Up until three weeks before the first round against Dublin, all of our training was done in water. I had gotten the idea because I'd read about Joan Benoit who won the gold medal in the women's marathon at the Los Angeles Olympics.*

Six weeks before that she had had an operation on her knee and did all her training in water. It was only 11 days before the race that she put her foot on the track for the first time, and she won the gold.

PADDY CULLEN

When I think of the first match, the ball hopped over the bar for an equalising point. I shouldn't be mentioning names here, but it is 25 years... so what the hell. Mick Deegan was soloing with the ball towards the Hogan Stand – all he has to do is kick it up into the upper deck, but he solos with the ball, and it gets tipped away. Gillick gets the ball, he is over by the Hogan Stand, he boots the ball in... and it bounces in the square and over the bar. It could have gone into the net, which would have been worse, but it bounced over the bar and that was how they drew that match.

In the second match, I keep mentioning names but he won't mind, Vinny Murphy... a great man, I had great time for Vinny Murphy. He got through with the ball in the last minute, all we needed was a point... 'Just fist it over the bar, Vinny!' I asked him afterwards, and he said, 'Paddy, when I see the goal... I go for it!'

In the third game, Paul Clarke had the ball. We had worked the ball up the field very well, just needed a point... and the game was over, and Clarke was about 35 yards... and Paul was fairly accurate but it went wide. And the fourth game, it was full of excitement, there was the penalty and Mick Lyons was inside the square... and you didn't know who was taking the penalty.

We missed the penalty and we still led by six points with 11 minutes to go.

In the last game too, Bernard Flynn beat John O'Leary to a ball. Now we all know Bernard Flynn, he is not a big man... but he got to a ball before John got to it and it went into the net. I am not blaming John O'Leary.

I was a goalkeeper myself and we all know my incidents in the past, but those little things happened. When you look back on them and you think if only... if only he had kicked it into the stand, if only he had kicked it into the canal. If only...

SEÁN BOYLAN

After the first match the county board said to me, 'Do you want to take the players away anywhere?' And I said we were fine.

I was asked again after the second match, but said no again. But after the third one I went around to all the wives and girlfriends of the players and said, 'Listen, if I want to do something with the lads, would you mind?'

They were like, 'Seán, whatever it takes to beat the Dubs.'

Anyway, I got it into my head that we'd go to Scotland. Myself and our sponsor Noel Keating (MD of Kepak), God rest him, went across. David Beggy was working all over Scotland at the time and picked us up in a souped up Escort... and Noel, who was used to a big Merc, had his knees up on the windscreen. Jinksy was flying down the roads and smoking! Jesus, would you stop!

Anyhow, we head up towards Loch Lomond and came to a little village called Drymen and stopped to get a cup of tea in a place called The Buchanan Arms.

After five minutes, I said this is the place. Ironically it was where Billy Connolly is from. So we talked to the people and made the arrangements and came home and got the approval from the Meath County Board.

We hired a plane and all flew over on the Friday.

It had been non-stop between training, work, minding injuries and everything, so the very first night we had a five-course meal and a great chat afterwards... and a bit of music and so on.

We had to take the tension out of it, because at that stage there was very little you could learn about Dublin.

There's nothing like the anxiety of the moment to soak away your energy... and half the training I wanted to do over there was to simply absorb that tension.

The wise lads knew that the next day we'd be working, and we did. We went for a training session the next morning and then afterwards some of them went clay-pigeon shooting and some of them went out to Loch Lomond on boats.

Afterwards we had a bite to eat, looked at a video, and had a chat amongst ourselves.

The next morning was the Sunday morning and for the next 40 minutes, the only thing we did was move the ball... just like we did at the end of the fourth match against Dublin. Up and down... up and down the field.

So, for Kevin Foley to find himself right up at the Hill end and to be looking for the ball for that goal... that's exactly what we had worked on in Scotland, so in his head it was the most natural thing in the world.

PADDY CULLEN

He took them away to Scotland during the week coming up to the match and Seán Boylan believes (it made the difference). But I certainly don't believe it. In my estimation, it did nothing for them because they were six points behind with 10, 11 minutes to go… so it can't be, unless some magic wand or something, I don't know, came down on top of them.

But he reckons that's maybe what did it for them. I don't think so.

They got a break, you get them in life… something just happens and you get a break.

I thought the referee Tommy Howard did really well in those games. 'Hopper Howard' we called him, because he hopped the ball so much! But he handled the games really well. It was exciting stuff. There was hitting but it was generally fair.

It was the way football was meant to be played.

That's the way the game was made and he let it flow.

Everybody took the hits.

SEÁN BOYLAN

I suppose it's just knowing there's always time, things can change, and being ready for it. I always remember calling over Liam (Hayes) when Keith Barr was taking that penalty and telling him, 'Even if they score this, ye can still win it. Start throwing the ball around like you did in Scotland last weekend'.

Then in the last seven or eight minutes, the way they played was just magic. For Kevin Foley to score that goal… I remember poor Paddy Hickey interviewing him afterwards and asking him upside down and inside out about other scores… and how this compared to them. Kevin said he never scored for Meath. Paddy asked him about any he'd scored for his club, and Kevin said he'd never scored for his club. Paddy asked him about any he'd scored for his school, and Kevin said, 'Paddy, you're standing on my towel!'

PADDY CULLEN

David Beggy, who I know very well… for him to get the winning point, it is like an old woman getting a point from about 75 yards! I mean, if you were to put money on anyone getting the winning point, it wouldn't be David Beggy… and we have been laughing about it since. So, there are plenty of memories of those games, plenty of incidents you can pick out but there are also incidents with Meath that you can pick out. But we dominated the games, every game we dominated.

But you couldn't get rid of Meath… Meath were like that.

SEÁN BOYLAN

When Jinksy got that ball, there was never a doubt in my head but that he was going to put it over the bar. He could have gone for the safe option, but he had the balls to go for it. The emotions were extraordinary because it was like the end of a season. No matter what you did you were never going to hit the same highlight, and yet you were still involved in trying to win a Leinster title.

And, absolutely, there was sympathy for Dublin too.

I was gutted for them. Because it could so easily have been the other way. There were no winners or losers really.

Gaelic won in a big way. It was nearly incidental which team won on the scoreboard.

Things were never the same again. Imagine a big championship match on a Saturday?! Years ago people would have been saying, 'Ah Jaysus lads, there's cows to be milked!'

In gaelic up until then, it always had to be Sunday afternoon, but so many things were opened from there. It got rid of the attitude of, 'You can't do this… or you can't do that'.

Afterwards it became more like, 'How CAN we do this or that?'

And people who were never interested in the game were now, suddenly, fascinated with it. I think it was the third match that Jack Charlton and Maurice Setters walked down Clonliffe Road on their way to the match.

It was incredible.

That's how much it captured the imagination.

◄ ◄ ◆ ► ►

MICK DELANEY COMMENTED to me as we left the meeting, after the draw was initially made for the football championship, 'We may have to sell the offices we just bought in Portlaoise!'

Who was to know that it would take four games to separate two great teams, with crowds averaging 60,000 at each game.

Tom Loftus was the previous Dublin man to chair the Leinster Council. That was back in 1972. People have commented on the fact that it is surprising that Dublin did not have more people at the top table in Leinster. Some would say there was an anti-Dublin bias when it came to the election of officers.

It was the norm that the vice-chairman would become chairman after his three years. That did not happen when Pat McDonnell, a Dublin man, was vice-chair.

Looking back now, I must say I was honoured to be listed among some great men who chaired the Leinster Council over the years.

◄◄◆▷►

MICHAEL DELANEY

Jimmy succeeded Jack Boothman as chairman. He had made his mark on the committee before then. In the late-70s, he co-operated very quietly and efficiently with Andy Gallagher of Offaly to introduce an open draw in Leinster hurling. Until then, it was always a seeded draw and every final was Kilkenny v Wexford, with a few exceptions when Dublin got through to the Leinster final in 1960 and '61, and Offaly got through in 1969, when by co-incidence Jimmy Gray refereed that game.

From 1980 to '90, Offaly were in every Leinster final. This may never have happened only for Jimmy and Andy's initiative in getting this proposal through.

The wheel turned in the late-80s when Meath and Dublin were dominating Leinster. Those who supported an open draw in hurling were now wanting one in football as well. Jimmy took it on the chin and agreed to it, even though Dublin didn't like it.

So, an open draw became a reality in Leinster football as well. The draw was made in November 1990. We had just moved in to our new office in Portlaoise. We were the first provincial council to have our own office. This was set up by Jack Boothman and Jimmy Gray.

Anyway, when the draw was made, Dublin and Meath were drawn to play in a preliminary round.

We thought we were financially doomed, but we weren't to know that it would take four games to find a winner… and we were in the money. Jimmy was a one-man show.

He could persuade the council members that they had made a decision, but he already had it made. Jimmy had plans for the money. The first group to be rewarded were the two teams and they got £30,000 each for a holiday abroad.

This was a novel idea and was very much appreciated. He gave each of the 12 counties £20,000 each as a dividend in 1991. He wasn't very happy with how some of the counties used the money. Some stopped their own fund-raising.

So, the following year he reduced it to £15,000. He then gave a sizeable amount of money to various charities. He still wasn't happy with some counties' use of the money so, for year three, he decided to draw up a coaching plan and created field officers to coach and promote gaelic games.

It was based on population size, so Dublin got five field officers and every other county got one each. This was the start of the coaching scheme which has been so successful.

It came from Jimmy Gray's forward thinking.

In his inaugural speech he mentioned that one of his priorities was the amalgamation of the second level schools committees. He believed that Cumann na mBunscol was doing a good job and third level was okay.

He saw a lot of problems at second level.

His diagnosis of the problem was that Leinster colleges had two bodies running the one show... the Leinster Colleges Council and the Vocational Schools Board. Jimmy's vice-chairman was Albert Fallon from Longford and he was a secondary school teacher, so Jimmy was pushing an open door in this area.

After a lot of discussion, in-fighting, and disagreements, the two bodies agreed to amalgamate and become the Leinster Post Primary Council.

Years later, the other provinces followed our example. It has worked really well and second level games now are run on a professional basis and many more schools have come on board. Referring back to the Dublin/ Meath saga, isn't it ironic, that when the dust had settled, Meath went on to win the Leinster final and Jimmy presented the cup to the Meath captain, Liam Hayes, who is now involved in a big way in this production.

That wasn't the only time that Jimmy presented a Leinster final cup. In 2013, when Dublin defeated Galway in the Leinster senior hurling final, Martin Skelly was the Leinster chairman and he graciously got Jimmy to present the cup to the Dublin captain Johnny McCaffrey. Jimmy was deeply moved by the honour – it brought tears to his eyes. Jimmy is a great Liverpool supporter, as he had worked there in the past, and he knew I was a Manchester United fan, so he went ahead and organised a trip to Old Trafford. Jimmy had contacts everywhere but, on our first trip, Kevin Moran was the contact.

Jim King, Albert Fallon and I were delighted to get such a trip. I have gone on several more trips to Old Trafford with Jimmy. We went on a few day-trips as well. In due time, Joe Shaughnessy from Wexford joined our party. We would play a few games of golf in Wales and then head for Manchester.

He was marvellous company and had some wonderful stories. One story that sticks out… when he was refereeing a big game, he had his brother Dinny and Donal Hickey as umpires at one goal.

Donal gave a very dodgy decision at one stage.

Jimmy said to Dinny at half-time, 'I thought that ball was wide.'

'It was!' says Dinny, 'but I couldn't go against another Na Fianna man!' He was a fiery goalkeeper and didn't like forwards coming in on top of him. He was lucky to have such a good full-back line in front of him – Des Ferguson, Noel Drumgoole and Lar Foley. Even as Leinster chairman he could be very vociferous on the line. I recall one time Donal Hickey had to ask him to cool it.

He was very much in favour of supporting clubs and counties when they ran golf classics. He was of the belief that it was appropriate to support these classics by entering a Leinster Council team.

He was always available to play on those teams and, I must admit, that I played on many of them as well.

He is an extraordinary man and he made a wonderful contribution to the GAA. It was a pleasure to have worked with him and have him as a friend.

MICHAEL REYNOLDS

Jimmy Gray, as chairman of the Leinster Council, brought a business approach to the province. He treated it like a small business and duly acted accordingly.

The Leinster second level schools competitions were run by the secretary of the day, while the vocational schools worked away on their own. In the late-80s there was an application for a secretary to run the games.

When Jimmy became chairman he opted to go a different route and decided that the two bodies would come together as Leinster Post Primary and he appointed a full-time officer to run the games.

As luck would have it, I was appointed to the role with responsibility for second level games in the province. Jimmy appointed Albert Fallon as chairman of the new body. Albert was the ideal man for the position. He was a secondary school teacher, teaching in a convent school in Ballymahon, but the school teams took part in competitions organised by the Vocational committee.

After a lot of meetings and the lapse of a good few years, the other three provinces eventually adopted the Leinster model and it is now the Post Primary sector in all four provinces.

Jimmy's commitment to the project has paid off, as the Post Primary games are now run on a very professional basis. Jimmy was a driver of the Post Primary vision for the future and I can say, hand on heart, there hasn't been one accusation from one sector against the other. The members of the first Leinster Colleges Council were all nominated by their own sector and, after so many years, we were supposed to vote again but there was no need. 1991 gave us the four matches between Dublin and Meath, which brought in serious revenue.

As Leinster chairman he ensured that all counties in the province benefited from the revenue of those four games.

He was a very fair man and didn't suffer fools easily. Despite being 91, he embarrassed me last summer when he rang me up to see how I was getting on… when really I should have been ringing him. There was a lovely human touch to the man always.

When it came to the Dublin revolution, Jimmy succeeded in sailing the ship around rocks. If you want to rise him, start praising referees.

He was so passionate at games and the poor old referee as well as offending players were in the firing-line. He was the boss of transportation for the Sugar Company.

Jimmy clashed one night with Jerry White from Kerry, who accused Jimmy of trying to kill the vocational sector. Jimmy was furious at the allegation… and how he didn't go across the table still amazes me. He had all Leinster on his side, people like Peter Cashman and An Br Ó Fearghaíl.

He asked the good Brother one time was he doing the right thing? And the response was, 'It should have happened long ago'.

At a meeting one night, as it approached 10 o'clock, Jimmy said, 'I should be in Rotterdam at a meeting, but I decided that this was more important.'

Someone responded with, 'I should be in my bed now!'

Jimmy saw red and was not impressed by the lack of appreciation. He was so committed to the second level schools project that he was able to reschedule his meeting in Rotterdam.

Jimmy was a serious business man, and if you came looking for money with a cock and bull story, you'd get nowhere.

He would say, 'Where is your plan?'

He was very friendly with the public officer of Coca-Cola, Jim Whelan, a Wicklow man, whose brother Peter was an inter-county referee. I'm convinced that it was through their friendship that Coca-Cola sponsored Leinster Colleges for over 20 years.

Jimmy had great contacts and used them to great advantage. We got €25,000 a year which was serious money for schools competitions.

He made a comment one night at a meeting to the members... 'You are entitled to know what the staff members earn. If you wish to know... see me privately'.

Nobody went to him, but he could never be accused of not giving them the option. Governance was a strong point with him.

When the clock approached 10.30pm at a meeting, Jimmy would say, 'I'm thirsty!'... which meant finishing and going to Casey's for a pint. But, all the important work had been dealt with by then.

He was a very strong chairman and he earned everyone's respect.

JOHN HORAN

Jimmy is an inspiration to everybody in Na Fianna.

He was a great man to get jobs for people. He had a wonderful GAA network. He sat at the corner of the bar at night time and I often sat there beside him.

One clear memory I have of him is, he taking a beer mat and writing down things he had to do for people... 'Jimmy, could you do me a favour.'

It was like as if he was running a constituency clinic.

Certainly, I learned a lot from him, especially about the politics of the GAA. He knew how it worked. He was invaluable to me when I was going for chairman of the Leinster Council and for president of the GAA.

He was always in the background offering advice. When I returned to the club after being president, I said that I might have been the first president of the GAA from Na Fianna... but Jimmy Gray should have been the first.

He is a wonderful clubman.

He was, and is, a great supporter of all the teams in the club. He is so positive about everything and it was always Na Fianna... Na Fianna. The amount of voluntary work that he has done over the years is phenomenal.

After serving brilliantly as county chairman he returned to the club, became chairman there and managed teams. He was very committed to the underage structure especially, linking up with local schools.

He always viewed that as extremely important to the club. That's where I got involved with Jimmy, when I joined the club. He is totally inspirational to everybody in Na Fianna. And in spite of his age, he is still going to games and supporting club and county.

He turned up in Carlow for a Walsh Cup match on one of the worst nights we ever had back in 2018. You wouldn't put a cat out that night.

He became Leinster chairman in the early-90s and he was possibly unlucky not to become president of the GAA. It was in a different era.

The GAA was probably at that time a more conservative body. Some people would have been afraid of his business man's ideas.

The respect they have for him is key to it all. Bringing in Kevin Heffernan to manage Dublin in the 70s, and scaling back the number of selectors to three was huge. It brought Dublin back and it brought crowds back. It also made gaelic football attractive again and the Dublin/Kerry rivalry was exactly what the game needed.

It was Jimmy's decision to put Heffernan in charge.

Jimmy also used his business background to manage Dublin and Leinster. He was ahead of his time and nearly all clubs and counties use that business model now to run their affairs. He was twice a trustee of the association as well.

He was definitely a president that the GAA missed out on.

◄◄◆►►

In his days as Leinster Council chairman, Jimmy was busier than ever before and enjoying the friendship of Dubliners and people around the country (above, Jimmy with future Taoiseach Bertie Ahern and Kilkenny goalkeeping great Noel Skehan). His service to Dublin and the province also saw him inducted into the Gaelic Greats Hall of Fame, when he was honoured by Leinster chairman Seamus Howlin in 2010.

« CHAPTER 11 »

Bainisteoir

I WAS SURPRISED, in 1993, to be asked to go for the position of manager of the Dublin senior hurling team. John Bailey was chairman at the time and he had asked Kevin Heffernan to recommend suitable candidates for all team manager positions.

So, Kevin rang me one day.

He said he would meet me in Clontarf Golf Club on the following Monday night. When we met as planned, he informed me that he wanted me to take over the position of manager of the senior hurlers. Now, Dublin senior hurling wasn't a very exciting project at that time. I told him I felt I was too old… and I wouldn't have the enthusiasm needed for such a role. He told me not to make any decision and that we would meet again in a week's time.

As the week went on, I began to like the idea of being manager.

I met him again as agreed, and told him I would accept the offer and I thanked him. 'Not at all,' he said, 'We couldn't get anybody else anyway!'

That would be Kevin's sense of humour.

LAR FOLEY AND his back-room team of Seán Shanley and Mick Kennedy had been there for the previous five years. They reached two Leinster finals in that period. In 1990 they lost to Offaly on a scoreline of 1-19 to 2-11. They had a great win over Wexford in the semi-final. That was one of our best performances and hopes were high that the corner had been turned. Vinny Holden and Shay Boland were outstanding in defence, and up front Ciarán Hetherton, MJ Ryan and Brian McMahon were in great form.

But sadly, a few weeks later, we were back to our usual inconsistent form.

The score difference of only five points didn't reflect Offaly's dominance on the day. Lar Foley was quoted afterwards as saying, 'We are still learning and have a lot more to learn if we are to win a Leinster title again'.

In 1991, Kilkenny defeated the Dubs by two points in the Leinster final. Dublin had a great win over the Leinster champions Offaly in the semi-final. Again, we looked sharp and well deserved a win. John Twomey had an outstanding game in defence and Seán Kearns and John Murphy won the midfield battle, and up front MJ Ryan and Seán McDermott got the crucial scores.

Their final performance was much better than the previous year, and it took a great save by Michael Walsh in the last few minutes to guarantee a Kilkenny win. Even though they were beaten, things looked brighter for Dublin. Sadly, the next three years we exited the Leinster Championship... losing to Wexford on each occasion.

Lar Foley stood down as manager in 1993 due to illness. His brother Des joined Seán Shanley and Mick Kennedy for the remaining few games.

I was appointed manager and my backroom team was Seán Buckley, manager of club champions St Vincent's and Paddy Maycock from Crumlin... and Mickey Whelan was our trainer. We had wins over Clare. Offaly, and Meath in the league.

However, we will remember 1994 for all the wrong reasons.

We played Wexford in the Leinster Championship quarter-final at Nowlan Park on June 6. We hurled really well and were leading by 11 points early in the second-half. The game was turbulent from the start and, by the end of the game, four players had been sent off – Eamon Clancy and Shay Boland, and George O'Connor and Tom Dempsey.

Wexford got back into the game in the second-half when they moved Martin Storey from centre-forward to midfield. We had Liam Walsh at centre-back and he kept Storey very quiet in the first-half. We probably should have sent Liam out to midfield to follow Storey. We are always wiser in hindsight.

Wexford outscored us 3-4 to 0-4 in the final 17 minutes.

They equalised with time running out. We went a point up again, but Storey earned a draw with another point. The Leinster Council took swift action and suspended five players – Clancy, Boland, McKeown, O'Connor and Dempsey. Both counties were fined £7,000.

It was one of the biggest fines ever imposed on hurling teams.

WE WERE AFRAID that we may have missed the boat in not winning the first day.

We brought in Brian Kelleher for the replay. Wexford were a different team. Brian struggled to mark Billy Byrne, who scored 2-2. Liam Dunne got the upper-hand on Ciarán Barr and John Twomey. All over the field, we were playing second fiddle.

The only players who showed some form were Conor McCann, Brian McMahon, Andy O'Callaghan and Liam Walsh. It was a very disappointing way to exit the championship.

We lost to Kerry, Waterford and Down in the league games played in the autumn. Our only win was against Carlow.

We had a promising start to 1995 when we defeated Wexford and drew with Meath and Offaly. However, we did not qualify for the final stages of the league and that was a big disadvantage as we lacked real competitive games in preparation for the championship. We decided that it was time to bring some new players on board.

We had seven players who made their debuts in Croke Park against Kilkenny – Brendan McLoughlin, Seán Deignan, Vinny Murphy, Shane Cooke, Paddy Brady, Mick Morrissey and John Small. We got a good beating on the day on a scoreline of 4-13 to 2-10. Our best players were the veteran John Twomey, Ruairi Boland, Liam Walsh, Paddy Brady and Seán Deignan.

I remember talking to Paddy Downey of *The Irish Times* after the game and he wasn't impressed by our performance. He wrote the following morning in his paper that the followers who patronised the game… Would have derived more enjoyment and excitement had they stayed at home, or anywhere, watching paint dry.

A bit tough, I think, and it doesn't do justice to the hard work of so many people. But journalists call it as they see it, I presume.

So, we headed into our final year of management and had a very poor start losing to Antrim, Laois and Westmeath, which meant a return to Division 2 for the following year. We decided to bring in some more debutantes for the championship. We had Eamon Burke in goal, Damien McCormack in defence, and Kevin Flynn, Eamon Morrissey, Gerry Ennis, Jamesie Brennan and Stephen Perkins in attack.

Morrissey and Brennan had won All-Ireland medals with Kilkenny in 1992 and '93. They had recently joined O'Toole's. We hoped they would make a big difference for us, and they did, but not immediately. As soon as Wexford identified the threat of Eamon Morrissey, they moved Larry O'Gorman back from centre-back to mark him and they took over from then... they won easily.

Needless to say, we were disappointed with how our three years had gone, but at least we felt we introduced some new hurlers to the scene and they played a big part in the ensuing years.

I was personally delighted that the powers-that-be decided to change the format so that the defeated Leinster finalists would be allowed into the All-Ireland quarter-final. It guaranteed another game, and might have made a big difference to Lar Foley in 1990 and '91.

◄◄◆►►

SEÁN BUCKLEY

When we were asked to come on board we were aware that it would be a tough task. Jimmy Gray, a mad hurling man, convinced me to join himself and Paddy Maycock on the management team.

I was thinking back about those years a while ago, and I remember well the game versus Wexford in Nowlan Park. We played really well and built up a decent lead. The game eventually ended in a draw. Now we got beaten the next day.

But we were only a puck of a ball away from beating Wexford, who were All-Ireland champions two years later. Wexford got a hell of a fright but they were ready for us in the replay. I met the Wexford manager after the game and I knew by him that he was delighted to get a second chance. Who knows what would have happened if we got the big break the first day. I would have been so proud if we had won that day in my own county of Kilkenny.

Dublin hurlers were looked down on by other hurling counties then, and took them as easy targets. I suppose that gets to you and some players mightn't be as committed as they should. But I must say that the players we had then gave it their best shot and they were a joy to work with. We had a lot of young players on that team and it takes time to get your game up to inter-county level.

Mickey Whelan was brilliant as trainer. The players looked up to him and he is such a wonderful character... he has such a grá for the hurling.

We had a lot of good players like Liam Walsh, Shay Boland, Brian McMahon. Brendan McLoughlin, Seán Power and John Murphy. Liam was a good player but could have been a great player if he wasn't so laid back. Then he dabbled in football. He was a great man for the craic. Conor McCann came on later and had massive potential. Brian Kelleher from Ballyboden was a serious full-back.

Then, of course, we had two All-Ireland medal winners in Eamon Morrissey and Jamesie Brennan. From my own club, StVincent's, we had Eamon Clancy, Ciarán Barr, Shane Dalton, Seánie McDermott and Paddy Brady. You know, it is so hard to improve when you only have one match every summer. It was a crazy system and I cannot fathom how the GAA did allow such a system to prevail for so long.

The big question, of course, is how come a team can be so good one day and so poor the next day? You saw it again recently, when Dublin met Kilkenny in the semi-final in Croke Park. Kilkenny went in at half-time 14 points up and Dublin fans were afraid of what would happen in the second-half. However, Dublin came out and totally controlled the half and brought the lead down to one point... and could have won it on the night.

I would dearly love to see Dublin winning an All-Ireland, because so much good work is done by schools and clubs. Dublin needs to keep working away, providing the best coaches they can get to look after the teams. Dublin clubs are really working hard and the county board gives all players plenty of matches every year.

There is a massive growth in the numbers playing hurling and the skill level is much improved. So, hopefully the reward of a Liam MacCarthy will come sometime soon to Dublin.

◄◄◆▷►

In the mid-90s, Jimmy succeeded his former teammate and great friend Lar Foley as Dublin senior hurling manager.

« CHAPTER 12 »

Friendship

I FEEL VERY blessed to have been so involved in the GAA all my life.

It has given me some wonderful memories. I have enjoyed some great victories and some sad defeats. But that is life. I have come across some wonderful people during my time and I could fill a good few books if I mentioned them all.

However, a few stand out and I am privileged to have known them and call them my friends. Most of them have left us and are gone to their eternal reward.

JIM BOGGAN

I FIRST GOT to know Jim Boggan when Br Cody and himself trained and managed the Dublin minor hurling team to win the 1965 All-Ireland final. They had a great win over a very strong Limerick team. Br Cody was a Kilkenny man teaching in St Vincent's in Glasnevin, and Jim was involved with St Columba's, who were very strong in hurling at the time.

I met Br Cody sometime after the All-Ireland final. 'If you ever are in a position to choose team managers,' he said to me, 'make sure Jim Boggan is not lost to hurling. He was the major contributor to our win!'

Jim was born in Wexford and his parents decided to move to Dublin. He got involved with the St Columba's club... they were a great hurling club and Jim became an integral part of that club. Before long, he got involved with county teams too, and had success at minor and under-21 level. He managed the Dublin seniors a few times and, while never winning a major title, he always improved the standard of hurling – and the players always appreciated his commitment and enthusiasm.

I was involved as a selector with him and he always spoke his mind... everybody knew where they stood with Jim. In the early-90s, he managed the Dublin senior camogie team for three years, when my daughter Carmel was playing for the county.

He believed strongly in the idea of playing Dublin-born players *only* on county teams. There were a lot of good players from other counties playing club hurling in Dublin but Jim always felt it would be better, in the long term, if only Dublin-born players were considered.

When I retired from the Sugar Company, I started a small business myself.

I was looking around for a small premises in the city and I happened to mention it to Jim. Now Jim had an office over the Busman's Union in Parnell Square. When I told him it would only be myself and a part-time assistant, he told me I could have a desk in his office and his two assistants Ruth and Susanne would be more than willing to help in any way they could. So, I took up the offer. I had a successful little business and Jim kept me straight on the financial side... and the two ladies were most helpful. I will always be eternally grateful to Jim for his kindness and generosity.

He was a major contributor to the Paul Mulhere Benevolent Fund, which was a great success and helped a lot of young people as they prepared for working life.

The Friends of Dublin Hurling made Jim the first recipient of the Lar Foley Hall of Fame Award. As it was one of our first big nights at the Red Cow Moran Hotel, we were anxious that everything went well. Over 350 people were booked in. It was well known that Jim didn't like the limelight and there was genuine concern that he mightn't turn up to receive the award. So a plan was concocted involving the Crumlin club and ourselves.

Jim was told that I was getting the award, and that I would be honoured if he would attend. He agreed to attend with some of his Crumlin friends. We had a lot of awards on the night and Jim's Hall of Fame was to be the last one. Halfway through, word was sent to the top table that Jim was planning to leave.

So we changed the order of awards and went ahead with the big one. It went really well, and while embarrassed with all the attention, I think he enjoyed it. It was a fitting honour for such a wonderful, humble man.

As well as everything else, Jim was a social worker and he was deeply committed to the less well off in life, and helped an awful lot of people. His untimely death in 2009 shattered us all, and he was a great loss to Dublin hurling.

He was a legend in the Crumlin area.

JIM KING

JIM WOULDN'T HAVE survived nowadays. He did *everything*. He was secretary and treasurer, and much more as well.

Jim lived off the South Circular Road. He had a little bar in his front room and his neighbour, the great Luke Kelly, would often call in for a drink. He was a wine salesman and, as a consequence, he was known by every priest in Ireland as he sold them altar wine. He was a founder member of O'Connell Boys GAA club.

They were linked to Belvedere College, who amongst many other projects, cared for some disadvantaged young people. In due time, Jim was the club delegate to the Dublin County Board. After a few years he was appointed secretary of the Minor Board. He graduated from there to become secretary of the Senior Board.

From 1970 onwards, the workload increased immeasurably. New clubs were founded, many more teams took part in competitions and it became too much to handle. Mick Leahy was assistant-secretary and a great help to Jim. Paula Lee was the office secretary and they were a wonderful team.

One day, Jim asked to see me for a chat.

We met the following day at the Gresham Hotel. He explained to me that they needed more help with the administration and that he had somebody in mind. When I asked him who he had in mind he said, 'He is a young fella and he is the Erin's Isle delegate to the board. His name is John Costello'.

Jim made many big calls in his time, but this one has to be his best. John replaced Jim and is now our CEO for the past 25 years and he has done a marvellous job, and is rated as one of the top GAA officials in Ireland. He is responsible, more than anybody, for the successful Dublin story.

Jim kept his cards close to his chest and he ran the business in a very efficient way.

I only got to know him really when I became county chairman, although I was aware of his work as Minor and Senior Board secretary. I must say that at that time I thought him to be a bit dour and distant, and certainly not one to get on the wrong side of. In fact, my first kind of contact with him was when I had the temerity to raise at a county board meeting the lack of support there was for the senior hurling team.

I remember well the episode.

Dublin had played Wexford in a Walsh Cup match in Wexford Park. When the time came to go out on the pitch it was discovered that there were no spare hurleys, and we had to borrow some from the opposition. Needless to say, there were many unkind words about the board and its secretary, and Christy Hayes and myself were delegated to raise hell at the next board meeting.

This we both did, with indignation, and the worst part of the whole saga was that we were allowed rant on before the horrible truth came out. Jim announced, calmly, that if somebody had taken the trouble to look, they would have found a dozen hurleys... in the boot of the bus.

He did the accounts as well as everything else and he minded every penny as if it was his own money. He didn't like any wastage and he queried many a bill.

Two stories come to mind in that regard. When I was manager of the senior hurling team in the early-90s I brought the team to Limerick for a weekend as we prepared for the Leinster Championship. We played Eamonn Cregan's club Claughaun on the Saturday evening and we played Limerick on the Sunday.

We stayed overnight in the beautiful Woodlands Hotel in Adare. The following Sunday we played Meath in a Walsh Cup game in Trim. I visited Jim in hospital early the following week and, after the usual salutations, he inquired if we had any game on the Sunday? I told him we had and that we won fairly easily.

His only comment was, 'Did ye stay overnight?'

The second story is about the famous 1977 All-Ireland semi-final against Kerry. It was rated, and indeed still is rated, as being the best football match ever played and this was the theme of all the reports and commentaries on the game. When you are close to the team, as we were, you don't appreciate how good or how bad it is.

In the week following the match, I said, 'It must have been a great game, Kinger?'

'I suppose it was!' he said.

Before adding... 'It cost us seven jerseys!'

As is often the case, in the situation of a county chairman and his secretary, we had our differences, but Jim being *Jim*, he went by the book, no matter what. Jimmy Keaveney had been sent off in a club match and on the anticipated referee's report, it looked like he was going to get a month's suspension.

We were discussing this seriously because there was an important Dublin match coming up. I felt that perhaps one of us should contact the referee, and ask that he might look favourably on the matter... so Jimmy would only get two weeks.

'Well, I'm certainly not going to do it!' he said.

I made the call, and Jimmy got two-weeks on the generosity of the referee. When this emerged, Jim said to me, 'You know Gray... you couldn't lie straight in bed!'

He was a very good friend of mine and we had many happy times together particularly in the 70s, on the trips in America and around the country. I was delighted he came on the All Star trips because there was so much work to be done to ensure a safe and successful tour. He was fiercely pro-Dublin, really to the extent of being paranoid about it.

He would give out privately about the players for one reason or another... it usually had to do with tickets, but he would defend them to the hilt against any criticism. He was very proud of that team.

Jim's great party piece was *Dicey Reilly* and, on rare occasions, was known to give rousing renditions of that old ballad.

He told me a story about his new bicycle.

One night he parked it outside the club. Not having a lock he felt that given the area, it wasn't too safe and asked this young lad to mind it for him. Alas, when he came out it was to discover that his bike had disappeared and, indeed, so had his minder. He called up to this 'latchico's' – a great expression of his – house and between one thing and another found the bike there.

Jim was incensed and, wondering whether to clatter him or hand him over to the police, decided to give him a lecture and have him suspended from the club.

'Ah please, Mr King, don't do that... give us a bar of *Dicey Reilly*'.

It is not easy to capture the character of Jim, because he was a very private person and while he had a wide circle of acquaintances, his circle of friends was small. There is one aspect of his life, however, which manifested itself most of all and that was his great kindness and generosity.

I had the privilege of giving the eulogy at his funeral. I mentioned his many acts of kindness to many people. As I was leaving the graveyard, I was approached by a gentleman who introduced himself.

'Mr Gray, you were right in what you said about Mr King,' he began. 'I was an orphan and I wasn't happy with the family that looked after me. Mr King was so good to me for so many years. I owe him so much.'

What a beautiful tribute.

KEVIN HEFFERNAN

MANY WOULD SAY that Kevin Heffernan was Dublin's best footballer of all time. His achievements are many, and I have already documented a substantial portion of them earlier in this book. He played minor hurling and football in the early-40s. He won a Leinster minor football medal in 1946 and, the following year, he won a Leinster minor hurling medal. He made his senior debut for the Dubs the same year he was sitting his Leaving Certificate exam.

He broke his jaw during his debut game just a few days before his first exam. He won three National Football League titles in 1953, '55 and '58, and he captained Dublin when they defeated Derry in the '58 All-Ireland Football final. He won two more Leinster titles in 1959 and '62. He made 115 appearances and he scored 52 goals and 115 points.

He was equally successful while playing for St Vincent's. He won a total of 15 Senior Championship medals. He won seven in-a-row from 1949 to '55 and he won six in-a-row from 1957 to '62. Vincent's changed the style of club football and made it a moving game rather than just 'catch and kick'.

Kevin was a dual player and he won six hurling championship titles in 1953, '54, '55, '57, '59 and '62. He would have walked onto the Dublin senior hurling team if he hadn't decided to concentrate on football.

If we had him in 1961, I feel we could have defeated Tipperary.

While he made a name for himself on the playing fields, of course he is best known for his role as manager of the Dublin senior football team.

As Heffo!

In 1974 Dublin won their first of four All-Irelands in the space of 10 years. 'Heffo's Army' was born, and a new culture was founded and it is still in place 50 years later. Three more titles followed in 1975, '77 and '83.

Even when his playing days were over he was still being honoured for his outstanding achievements. In 1974, after leading Dublin to winning the All-Ireland final, he was the only non-player to be honoured with the Texaco Footballer of the Year. In 1984 he was named as left corner-forward on the GAA's Team of the Century. In 1986 he managed Ireland to defeat Australia in the Compromise Rules series. In 1999 he was named as right corner-forward on the Team of the Millennium. In 2005 he was granted the Freedom of the City of Dublin.

All 100 percent deserved!

Even though I knew him for over 50 years, I could never say I knew everything about him. He was hugely intelligent and he had a serious job in the ESB. He would do anything for you as he was a most generous man. You would never get to know much about his family. His father was a policeman, and he never saw Kevin playing football or hurling. He had brothers and sisters, but I knew *nothing* about them.

He introduced Brian Mullins at the age of 18 and we all thought he was mad. When he introduced Bernard Brogan S nr, we all thought he was definitely losing it as Bernard didn't seem to be at that standard. One day he put Bernard on at half-time to play midfield with Brian Mullins.

Jim King said to me, 'Do you see what he is after doing… he's putting Bernard Brogan on!' Jim thought it was not going to work. Anyway, Bernard had a stormer and became a great Dublin player for years afterwards. Kevin could see things that the rest of us couldn't. I suppose, that's what separates the greats from the average.

Again, we couldn't believe when he brought in Mick Holden 10 days before a Leinster final. Even Mick's clubmates were taken aback. But it worked out and Mick did a wonderful job for the team. Mick was absolutely fearless and that's what Heffo saw in him. When he asked me to contact Mick, I was afraid that he might be a loss to the hurlers and I was sure Mick wouldn't make it.

Kevin made an enormous contribution to gaelic games. If I ever asked him to give a talk or make a presentation, he never once refused.

One summer the ground was extremely hard in Parnell Park and Heffo mentioned it to Lorcan Redmond. The following night, Lorcan noticed that the pitch was much softer even though no rain had fallen. When he inquired further he heard that Heffo himself was out at 5am and, with the help of the sprinkler system from Clontarf Golf Club, he did it himself.

He was old fashioned in many ways.

He loved his own company and you would often find him on his own, reading the paper and smoking his cigarette. We played Kerry in London one year, and the night of the game we were heading out to see some of the sights.

As we approached Piccadilly, Kevin announced, 'I'm off lads!' And he went off for a walk and then back to the hotel.

He was an extraordinary man and Dublin will be forever indebted to him.

DES FOLEY

HAVING ATTENDED THOSE two great nurseries of the GAA, Scoil Mhuire, Marino and St Joseph's, Fairview, Des learned well from his mentors, the Christian Brothers and teachers.

He showed his class when helping his school, St Joseph's Fairview to win the All-Ireland Colleges football final in 1959. He was the star performer in all the games leading up to, and including, the final.

Kevin Heffernan, in an interview with Dermot Gilleece, a fellow Joey's boy, spoke glowingly of Des. 'I remember the 1959 Hogan Cup final as a classic exhibition of all the qualities that characterised Des as a sportsman. The use of his God-given gifts of size and athleticism, his sportsmanship and the fact that he possessed an extraordinary Rolls Royce-engine that enabled him to travel with ease from a defensive role on our goal-line… to create havoc in an opponent's square.

'His presence was like a reservoir of confidence to the guys who played with him, travelling the length of the field, exhorting everyone to effort – and finally succeeding. Des was a huge presence in any company. When you put these attributes alongside his athleticism, his very keen eye and his indomitable will to win, you had a sporting colossus.'

Des played his club hurling and football with St Vincent's. His achievements include… 10 Senior Football Championships, four Senior Hurling Championships, three Minor Hurling Championships, two Minor Football Championships, and one Leinster Senior Club Championship.

He was equally successful when playing for his beloved Dublin.

His achievements include an All-Ireland Senior football medal, three Leinster senior football medals, one Leinster senior hurling medal, three Railway Cup football medals, two Railway Cup hurling medals... and a unique double, winning Railway Cup hurling and football medals in 1962 on the same day. He played midfield on both teams and turned in star performances. He also won two All-Ireland minor football medals, and was selected on both Ireland teams, hurling and football, in 1962 and '63. He captained two Dublin All-Ireland winning teams... minor in 1958 and senior in '63.

He had a life-long passion for St Vincent's and having given outstanding service as a player, he became a successful coach to players at all levels. When Lar got sick in the early-90s while managing the Dublin senior hurling team, Des stood in and took over the team until the end of the championship.

Des was such a quiet man.

Lar and himself were like chalk and cheese. Lar never stopped talking on the pitch, giving out, warning people and causing confusion.

Des, on the other hand, was never in any rows on the pitch. In my humble opinion, he was a better hurler.

He was very strong and could score... left or right, from any part of the pitch. Lar and Des were very close and if you looked crooked at Des, Lar would arrive in case punishment needed to be handed out. Mick Dunne had a programme on RTE and one night Paddy Grace, the Kilkenny secretary and myself were guests.

Now Paddy was very much into Kilkenny and you had to be exceptional to warrant praise from Paddy. Anyway, he made a statement that night saying that the best centrefield player he ever saw after Lory Meagher... was Des Foley of Dublin. That was some praise coming from Paddy.

After his Leaving Cert, he went into Freaney's Accountancy firm but he left after a year as it wasn't for him. He went back to the farm and worked with Lar, running their big farm and a farm machinery hire company. They were two extremely hard workers and, on the day of a game, they could be up at five in the morning to get everything done before heading off to play hurling or football for Vincent's or Dublin.

They had lights on their farm machinery so they could work very early in the morning or late into the night as required.

Des stood for election as a Fianna Fáil candidate. Kevin Heffernan was his election agent. One night a few of us went out to Lucan to canvass for Des.

Lar was one of the group. We went to this house in a small cul de sac and a lady opened the door and, when Lar told her he was the brother of Des, she invited us in for a cup of tea. She asked us could we guarantee that she would get running water if Des was elected. She went on and on, and Lar was getting cheesed off.

'I'll tell you mam!' says Lar, 'If he doesn't do it, I will come out myself and do it for you!'

There is a story that Des, on the day of the 1963 All-Ireland football final, spent the morning on the combine harvester, went to Croke Park, played a blinder for the team, won the All-Ireland… and returned home after the game and went back cutting corn.

On St Patrick's Day 1962, when Des became the first man to win Railway Cup medals in both hurling and football, he later referred to that achievement. 'It was one of the lucky things that happened to me during my career. People regard it as a fabulous achievement and perhaps it was, but at the time it didn't seem to be anything extraordinary.

I could only do it because I had fellas around me. I had a sore throat and a slight cough and I remember my mother giving me raw quinine… and it was like eating seaweed. I never thought of the football game during the first match. Mick Kennedy of Faughs had an absolute blinder that day. There was very little time between the football and the hurling so I had to race into the dressing-room for a quick wash.

'I then changed my togs and put on a new Leinster jersey and, while I was doing all this, the footballers were parading around the field.'

He played senior hurling for Dublin at the age of 18, which was unusual in those times. He turned in a huge performance for us in the 1961 All Ireland hurling final.

Heffo always said you need brains, courage and skill to make it at the top level at football. When it comes to hurling, I think the order is… skill, brains and courage. Des had it all.

As a player and captain, 'Desser' had few equals. He was fearless and possessed outstanding skill at both games.

However, it was his outstanding quality of true friendship that all who knew him will remember him by.

LAR FOLEY

LAR, LIKE HIS younger brother Des, started his schooling at Scoil Mhuire Primary School, Marino, and St Joseph's Secondary School, Fairview. 'Joeys' was building a strong hurling and football tradition and Lar was in his element in that school.

He joined the famed St Vincent's at an early age. There is little doubt that if there had been an All-Ireland club series in the 50s, St Vincent's would definitely have taken some honours. They had lots of top class players on their teams; people like Kevin Heffernan, Snitchy Ferguson, Norman Allen, Ollie Freeney, just to mention a few. Lar won 12 senior football titles with his club. He won six in-a-row from 1957 to '62, then he won three more in 1964, '66 and '67 and he won his final three from 1970 to '72. The All-Ireland Club Championship started in 1970 and in '73 St Vincent's met Nemo Rangers in the final. The game went to replay and Nemo ran out winners. Lar came on as a sub in both games.

Lar first wore his Dublin jersey as a minor footballer in 1955, winning an All-Ireland title when defeating Tipperary. The following year they repeated the success with a win over Leitrim. In 1958 he was corner-back on the team that won the All-Ireland senior football final with a narrow win over Derry. Five years later, he got his second All-Ireland football medal as a full-back when Dublin defeated Galway.

He was awarded Texaco Footballer of the Year in 1963. He was also a dual player and he won four senior hurling club titles, in 1957, '60, '62 and '64.

He was right corner-back for the Dublin senior hurlers from 1961 to '66. He had the misfortune of being sent off in the 1961 All-Ireland final after Snitchy Ferguson had been hit by Tom Ryan, who had just come on as a sub, and Lar moved across to confront Tom. The ensuing skirmish led referee Jerry Fitzgerald to dismiss both players. It was most unfortunate, as Lar was a much greater loss to Dublin than Tom was to Tipperary.

He represented Leinster hurlers on three occasions and won two Railway Cup medals, in 1962 and '64.

Lar eventually retired as he was trying to manage a big farm and a young family. He continued to help out with his club in a coaching capacity. In 1990 he was appointed manager of the Dublin senior hurling team. He reached two Leinster finals in his three years and had a really good team but the old problem of inconsistency cost them a precious title. He had a massive passion for Dublin hurling and he earned the respect of the players.

He was quoted once as saying, 'I honestly think we could have had a great team if everybody was available. I'd love to have the likes of Dessie Farrell available to me. Dessie was a great footballer but he had a great natural talent for hurling as well'. In view of all the discussion of player burnout, Lar had an interesting theory.

'Dublin needs to create a system whereby quality players are guaranteed a game every week. We used to play for Vincent's three times a week and we never needed to train. The games don't seem to be there anymore and there's too much emphasis on training and running.'

When Des died, well before his time, I went out for his removal and was sympathising with Lar. 'Des will be remembered as a great hurler as well as a footballer,' I remarked. 'I'm not sure what you will be remembered for?'

'I'll be happy if I am remembered as a good farmer,' Lar replied.

When The Friends of Dublin Hurling was set up in 2002, they named Lar as one of their patrons and he is remembered yearly when they announce their Lar Foley Hall of Fame winner.

There are many stories told about Lar. He was an uncompromising opponent and players did not like marking him. As hurling manager, he is reported as going into the dressing-room before a game and saying to his team, 'Here is a bag of 45 sticks and, at the end of the game, I just want to be left with kindling!'

He had a very kind heart as many people can attest to. I recall on one occasion on the way by train to a match, I was cribbing and moaning about the fact that I was away in Liverpool all week and couldn't get a chance to do a job on my front or back garden. Anyway, one morning the following week, my wife Gretta was talking to a neighbour and as they were chatting a tractor and trailer came around the corner.

The driver asked a neighbour, 'Where does Gray live?'

The neighbour pointed out my house. So, the tractor driver pulled up, took a rotavator off the trailer and started working on the front garden. Gretta thought I had hired somebody to do it. When he had all the weeds removed and the patch rotavated, and ready for seeding, he moved to the back and did the same.

When he had finished, he said to Gretta, 'There you are missus, you can tell the little fella… he can seed it himself!' It was Lar and his son.

Anytime I would call out to Kinsealy for a chat you would always find a bag of potatoes in your car when you were leaving. Lar was *big* in every sense of the word.

He was a pantomime. I just regret I didn't write down some of the stories about him. Sometimes in a pre-match talk, he would throw a ball down in the middle of the floor and all the players would be around in a circle looking at this ball.

Then Lar would say, 'What are ye looking at… that ball isn't going to come up to ye. Go and get it!'

At the half-time pep talk the players made sure not to be too close to Lar, as he would grab somebody's hurley and he would give a few swings showing what he wanted in the second-half and, if you were too close, you could get a clatter.

During my time as chairman, Vincent's were playing Civil Service, I think, in a championship match. A Vincent's spectator got hit by somebody and all hell broke loose. Lar was full-back for Vincent's and he was at the other end of the pitch away from the fracas. Anyway, Lar took off and was running down to sort it out.

So, I went out on the pitch.

'Lar don't go down there, go back to your position!' I told him.

'Jimmy, you are a friend of mine!' he replied, 'but get out of my f***ing way!'

Needless to say, I did that.

MICK HOLDEN

MICK HOLDEN WAS one of those players who made it look easy.

Training was never his favourite pastime. One of the many stories told about Mick is when they were training in O'Toole Park one dark evening. Jim Boggan was the manager. The session started with the usual four laps of the pitch. At the top end of the field was a roller for rolling the pitch. Mick would skip in behind the roller, smoke a cigarette and rejoin the group on the last lap.

His parents Tom and Josie were from Mullinavat in Kilkenny – hence their grá for the hurling. Mick's brothers PJ and Vinny gave outstanding service to Cuala and to Dublin over many years. Mick's sister Jo played camogie for Dublin, and Helen and Margaret were volleyball internationals. Margaret is the mother of Paul and Mark Schutte. The local Eblana CBS was a great promoter of hurling in those days and the Holden brothers were in their element.

Their father Tom was an inspiration to all sports fans in Dun Laoghaire.

Mick came up through the ranks and played minor, under-21 and senior, in hurling and football for his county. He was a member of the minor hurling team for four years… playing in goal for two years, and as a forward for the other two. He played for the Dublin under-21 football team in the All-Ireland final when they lost to Kerry in Tipperary Town.

Mick had been in New York for the previous two years and it was a big surprise to all when he got his place on the team, taking over from no less a man than Tommy Drumm. He played senior hurling for the county from 1977 to '82. He won a Railway Cup hurling medal in 1979 and he won a Railway Cup football medal in '85.

His call up to the senior football team in 1979 surprised everybody.

The Dubs had won five Leinster titles at this stage and Mick had not been part of the panel. He described the event best himself. 'One day the phone rang and this fella said he was Jimmy Gray, and he told me that Kevin Heffernan wanted me to come training with Dublin. I thought it was somebody messing.

'After all, it was not as if the season was just starting. The Leinster final against Offaly was just 10 days away. I put down the phone, but it rang again and it was actually Jimmy. So I went training. When the team was announced on Thursday night there was a gap at full-back but, on the Sunday, I got the No 3 shirt.'

Mick played senior football from 1979 to '85 during which time he got his All-Ireland medal in 1983 in that famous final versus Galway when Dublin were reduced to 12 players in the second-half and still won the game.

But Mick always preferred hurling.

He felt it was a better game. He won three Senior Hurling Championship medals with his club. After winning the 1979 Leinster football final which was played on a real hot day, Mick headed for Parnell Park to play for Cuala in the Dublin Championship semi-final. Most of the Cuala team were in Croke Park for the football final and some of them were suffering from the after-effects of the heat.

They were well beaten on the night by Crumlin but their best man was none other than Mick Holden. Mick was a very popular guy and his blond hair made him stand out. His brother PJ told me the story of Mick and his trips to New York to play football for Galway in the championship over there.

He got a ticket sent over for him to travel to play in the New York Championship semi-final. At the time he was working for the Royal Liver Insurance Company. He asked PJ and Vinny if they would do the collecting for him… and he promised to be back by Monday. So the two brothers agreed.

However, after winning his game on the Sunday, he decided to stay on for the final… and then stayed another week for the celebrations when they won. So PJ and Vinny had a room full of money when Mick got back home.

When we won the football final in 1983 Mick and some friends brought the Sam Maguire Cup around to the local schools. All the children were gathered in their hall to welcome the guests and, of course, to get a free class. When the formalities were over the teacher put his hand on Mick's shoulder and asked the pupils, 'Does anybody know this man?'

One young lad put up his hand and said, 'He's my grannie's insurance collector!'

Then there was the occasion at a team meeting before one big match when Heffo said he had some sleeping tablets for anybody who was nervous, and might have a problem sleeping, Mick put up his hand.

Heffo was more than surprised and said, 'Mick, you are the last person I would think has a problem sleeping'.

'They're not for me,' Mick replied. 'They're for my mother.'

Kevin Heffernan had a great admiration for Mick. Both were smokers and they had many a long chat over a cigarette. Mick was fond of a pint or two but, of course, they were off the drink leading up to big games. It is said that Heffernan would meet Mick on the eve of big games to ensure that Mick only had one pint before going to bed.

When we won the 1983 All-Ireland, the Cuala club held a function in the Royal Marine Hotel to honour Mick. Much to their surprise, Kevin Heffernan turned up during the night and said a few complimentary words about Mick. Afterwards, Kevin was chatting to a group of Cuala members and referred to Mick as a warrior.

'When you go to war, you need warriors on your side… and Mick was one brave warrior.'

On hearing of his sad passing on the morning of Wednesday September

26, 2007 Nickey Brennan, the GAA president said, 'Mick embodied that rare gift of being a gentleman who enjoyed every minute on the playing field, while performing in the hard edge of the cauldron of inter-county games!'

MICK LEAHY

MICHÉAL Ó LAOCHDHA DIED on October 24, 1996, at the age of 87 years, and with him died a part of old Dublin GAA. Just imagine what he saw from as far back as Bloody Sunday, through the 20s, 30s and 40s as a player... and the 60s, 70s and 80s as an administrator!

What a shame his memories and recollections were not recorded in some fashion because he was a marvellous story-teller, in his own inimitable way, and it would have given a very graphic insight to the evolution of the association in Dublin from those reasonably remote times to the ultra-modern days of the new Parnell Park and Croke Park

When I say that he was a great story-teller, I base this contention on my experience coming back from the Waterford Congress, when Mick and the late Eamon Malone were in the car with me. Both were reminiscing and regrettably the journey went by far too quickly because the stories just rolled on... from Bloody Sunday to the early days of Drumcondra soccer club.

But alas, we were back in Dublin too quickly and the whole thing ended.

Probably, the story of how he came to be in Croke Park on Bloody Sunday is one in itself and his telling of how he and his brother went to the game – and the events of the day – were so vivid that one could visualise very clearly what it was like.

As everyone knows, in the early hours of that morning Michael Collins' men executed the principals of the British Army Intelligence and as a consequence, retaliation in some form or another was expected, though certainly not in the form it took that day in Croke Park.

Mick's mother was not keen that they should go to the game and when they were boarding the train on the North Circular Road, she expressed her fears to the driver, who said, 'Don't worry mam, they'll be alright and couldn't be safer than in Croke Park'.

When the shooting started, Mick and his brother became separated in the ensuing panic. Eventually, two men lifted him over the boundary fence at the back of Hill 16, the fence being corrugated iron with spikes cut out at the top. He went up Joseph's Avenue and a woman came out of a house and brought him in to the front room where everyone was on their knees reciting the rosary.

Eventually, he made it home around midnight, as did his brother.

An interesting addendum to the story is that while the prayers were going on in the house one of the Dublin players in his football gear came in and joined in. However, shortly afterwards the military arrived and took him away. About 25 years later on, Mick was at a function given by the O'Toole's Club in Seville Place and, following a conversation with the person next to him, it transpired that he was the player who was taken away that day.

He was a great hurler, and a hurling man.

Mick, a very proud mentor of the Eoghan Ruadh's, won a Leinster Championship medal with Dublin. He was a regular member of the team and were it not for injury, he would have played in 1938, the occasion on which Dublin last won a senior hurling All-Ireland. He was naturally disappointed that he was unable to lineout in the final; he did, however, have the satisfaction of seeing his great Eoghan Ruadh clubmate Jim Byrne become the first and only Dublin-born man to win an All-Ireland senior hurling medal for his county.

He often told me he would have been the second Dublin-born player to have won an All-Ireland medal.

The Ruadhs had marvellous teams in those days and for a Dublin club competed with the best of the great 'country' teams like the Faughs, Young Irelands, New Irelands, and Erin's Own.

In fact they were beaten in four county finals in succession by the smallest of margins on each occasion, and on account of this the county board at the time presented them with a special set of medals. These are the recorded facts, but Mick told me once that the board really only handed over eight medals and those were to the players who played in all the four matches.

Eventually the Ruadh's won the championship, when they beat St Vincent's before a crowd of 20,000. Mick was club secretary then as well as a player.

Most people will be aware of the part he played in administration in Dublin. He was assistant-secretary and I think his happiest times in that capacity were in the 70s with the late Jim King. He was a very proud Dub, and I don't think that there was anyone prouder than he was of the 70s team.

His first love, above all else, however, was hurling and when he retired as a player he was often a selector on different teams, most notably in 1961 when we last contested an All-Ireland hurling final.

Mick had a fierce determination and an independent streak in him. He fought the Ruadh's case at the board and it didn't matter to him that he was an officer; if he felt the club needed support he certainly gave it.

There is also the story about the famous Leinster Championship medal that Con Martin never got, after winning the Leinster title with Dublin in 1942. Mick thought this was a terrible injustice and mentioned it to me many a time. Eventually, he proposed that the board present Con, however belatedly, with his medal. This was done 28 years later at a county board function – Con told me afterwards that of all the trophies and caps that he won, that medal was his proudest possession.

He was a wonderful man and Dublin GAA benefitted from his commitment and dedication.

NOEL DRUMGOOLE

ON JANUARY 9, 1995, Noel Drumgoole passed away quietly and peacefully at the Mater Private Hospital, thus bringing to an end all too prematurely the life of a unique and wonderful personality. To have had the privilege of playing with him, and also being a life-long friend, makes this appreciation both a bitter and sweet experience.

The bitterness stems from coming to terms with the passing of such a humble man, with so many special qualities, and exceptional achievements as an organiser, administrator and leader.

The sweetness is sourced in the memories, however, which come flooding back… games won and lost, his great sense of humour, his talent for telling a story and the special enjoyment he gained from stories told against himself.

Whilst all his achievements in a lifetime of dedication to Cumann Luthchleas Gael as a player, team manager, and administrator would be too numerous to list, there are a number that nevertheless deserve special mention. As a very young man in his late-twenties and due to the untimely passing of the legendary Colonel Coffey, Noel took on the onerous task as chairman of the St Vincent's Hurling and Football Club.

It was a most critical time in the club's history, involving the development of

Páirc Naomh Uinsionn at Raheny. Noel, though young in years and administrative experience, proved equal to the task, thus stamping himself as an individual with far-seeing and special qualities.

Noel had been a staunch full-back for Vincents and he won five county senior titles with them from 1953 to '60. He captained the Dublin senior team for a few years, winning a Leinster title in 1961, and running Tipperary to one point in the All-Ireland final of that year. He won three Railways Cup medals with Leinster and he captained them in 1962.

He was the founder and first chairman of the Na Piarsaigh Club in Limerick. He was so delighted to see it achieve senior status before he passed away. He would be so proud of their achievements over the last 30 years and, of course, they wear the old Dublin sky blue colours. Noel managed the Limerick senior hurlers from 1977 to '82, and again from 1985 to '86. Limerick were unlucky not to win an All-Ireland during those years, but they claimed two Munster titles and a National League during Noel's time as manager.

As chief organiser for the funding and building of the Mackey Stand at the Ennis Road Grounds in Limerick, the GAA was presented with one of the finest stadia in the country. These landmarks will always stand as monuments to his memory. Those of us who were close to him knew a man of honesty and integrity, and a never-ending pursuit of the ideal.

He was a man without bitterness, even though certain disappointments could have made him so. He met those twin imposters of both victory and defeat, and treated them just the same.

If Noel had a regret it had to be the defeat by Tipperary in the 1961 final.

From that fateful day, seven of his teammates have gone to join him on the playing field and council chamber of heaven... Christy Hayes, Des and Lar Foley, Fran Whelan, Paddy Croke, Achill Boothman and Snitchy Ferguson.

There is no doubt that if they are looking for a chairman, Noel will be the unanimous choice.

OLLIE FREANEY

IN DUBLIN FOOTBALL circles, Ollie was a legend and undoubtedly during his career he was by far the most loved and popular Dub of his time. From his boyhood days he was a centre half-forward and he made this position his own for close on 14 years with his beloved St Vincent's and Dublin.

During that time he was considered in the same class as Mick Higgins of Cavan and Seán Purcell of Galway and, in my opinion, he was the best 'forty yards man' that Dublin ever had before or since.

Ollie was born in Clontarf into a strong nationalistic family; his father a native of New Ross and his mother coming from the foot of the Comeragh Mountains. He was the second child in a family of two boys and two girls. His brother Cyril, some two to three years his junior, played with him for many years with club and county.

In 1945 he won a minor All-Ireland medal when Dublin beat Leitrim, and the following year he was picked for the senior team for the first time, at the age of 19. I remember him telling me that he made his senior debut in Drogheda versus Louth alongside such men as Paddy Bermingham from Saggart. When Paddy retired soon afterwards, Ollie made the centre-forward position his own and his senior career continued for some 13 years until the final of the Dublin Football Championship in 1959, when he captained Vincent's to victory.

During his football life he was never sent off the field for rough play or retaliation, despite the keenest provocation. Indeed, he heaped an amount of attention on his own shoulders by taunting his opponents with the odd snide remark… often times referring to 'knobbily knees' or 'cow dung on the boots'. This never endeared him to his opponents who might descend upon him in numbers… leaving Ollie's teammates unmarked, just as he planned.

His distribution was uncanny and very accurate. The 'punched pass' was the rule in the late-40s and 50s, and he was a past master at it. He was a great place-kicker too, but never a spectacular fielder. Nevertheless, he got loads of possession by luring his markers into the wrong position under the ball. Once in possession he was magically exciting and one could feel the buzz in the crowd with cries of… 'Come on Ollie, get them going!'

I will never forget his display against Cavan in the 1953 league final when he and 13 Vincent's colleagues demolished the All-Ireland title holders. Ollie's 'wile and guile' set the other forwards alight and Kevin Heffernan, Tony Young, Bernie Atkins, Des Ferguson and his brother Cyril responded brilliantly.

His first All-Ireland final appearance was in 1955 against Kerry. Dublin were captained by his life-long friend Denis Mahony at right full-back. They were beaten that year but the bould Ollie revived flagging hopes in the final quarter of the game by squeezing a 14-yards free into the net along the ground. The goalmouth was crowded with six massive Kerrymen, but Oliver somehow bamboozled them into letting a bobbily shot through for a goal.

Like Kevin Heffernan, whom he considered the best forward he ever played with, both men had a sixth sense on the field, each knowing where the other might be with uncanny accuracy.

On leaving school he studied Commerce in UCD and represented the Combined Universities team during those years. On graduation he qualified as a chartered accountant.

If Christy Ring of Cork was the best known hurler nationwide during the 50s, Ollie was the country's best known footballer. Though he had fewer All-Ireland titles than Christy! In 1958 Ollie won his only senior All-Ireland medal when Dublin beat a gallant Derry team in the final.

My family and I were on holidays in Longford, and I got a telegram from Jim King. There were no phones where we were, so I had to drive into Edgeworthstown. I phoned Jim and he informed me that he got a letter from the bank telling him not to write any more cheques.

Jim was on high doh about it, so I told him I would ring Ollie Freaney for advice. So I rang Ollie, and told him the story.

He was giving out like hell about the banks and their carry-on. He didn't like banks, by the way. He asked me to bring Jim and to meet him outside the bank the following day at 3pm. So, we met Ollie outside the Munster and Leinster Bank at the corner of O'Connell Street and Abbey Street. Ollie led us into the bank and, as we entered the main reception area, he said to a staff member, 'Where is the manager's office?'

She showed him the way, and Ollie headed straight for the door.

'Oh, he is busy at the moment… you can't go in. He has somebody with him!'

'He will have three people with him in a minute!' Ollie said. And he went straight to the door and into the office.

Ollie introduced himself and then produced the letter that Jim King had received. 'Are you the author of this letter?' he asked the manager.

'I am not the author, but I signed it,' said the manager.

Ollie proceeded to give a lecture to the manager on the importance of the

GAA and how all their affairs are guaranteed by Croke Park. Ollie went on and on, and the poor manager couldn't get a word in. Eventually, the manager said, 'Leave it with me!'

'I certainly will, but I will be back if necessary.'

Two days later we got a letter apologising for the inconvenience. As it transpired, we sold a piece of O'Toole Park and cleared the debt anyway. But Ollie was in his element, and Jim and myself just stood back and listened. He was some man.

Business-wise he was just as successful as on the football field, and possessed a quick brain and innate shrewdness. He set up and masterminded one of the largest accountancy firms in the country. Employing many GAA men and women who desired to follow that profession, his firm could at one time field a team in both hurling and football.

Married to Kathleen from Port-na Bláth in Donegal, Ollie was the proud father of five girls and two boys. No family ever had a better father and he was consumed with passing on to them his deep faith in God, which he repeatedly maintained was life's greatest jewel. He was a deeply spiritual man of prayer with daily Mass, Holy Communion and nightly Rosary.

He was a wealthy man too, but he never flaunted it and was really happy when walking the land on his farm which he acquired in county Dublin or relaxing in the bosom of his family at home in Portmarnock.

He was a hard-headed businessman, but he was a sucker for a sob story and many a widow and 'lame dog' would vouch for his goodness. Ollie was a one-off, a special genius, and a great friend.

The life of Jimmy Gray has revolved around the GAA and great friendships. Here he is (above) with two of his best friends Joe Rowley and Norman Allen. And in the late-70s he lined out (Jimmy is bottom right in the front row) for a charity game in Croke Park, in a group including entertainers Tony Kenny and Luke Kelly, Niall Toibin and Maureen Potter, and old teammates Kevin Heffernan Des Foley.

« CHAPTER 13 »

Hurling Then, and Now

IT IS SUCH a long time ago, that I struggle at times to recall the details of some games. Two of our great reporters during my playing days were Peadar O'Brien and Mick Dunne. They had a different style of reporting but they always captured the atmosphere of the game and they reported accordingly.

I have picked out two games from quite long ago, over half a century! Imagine! One a sad memory.

The other a very happy occasion.

◄◄◆►►

1959 LEINSTER HURLING FINAL

By PEADAR O'BRIEN

KILKENNY 2-9   DUBLIN 1-11

Lucky Kilkenny! A last-second goal by their captain, Seán Clohosey, snatched victory from the closing jaws of defeat in this thrill-packed Leinster senior hurling final at Croke Park yesterday and carried the Noremen into yet another All-Ireland final.

With Dublin leading by two points, and the crowd awaiting the final whistle, Kilkenny were awarded a touch-line puck some 15 yards from the Dublin goal on the Cusack Stand side at the Canal End.

By my reckoning we were already 45 seconds into 'lost' time, as chunky Johnny McGovern sent the ball sailing right across the Dublin goalmouth. There was a clash of hurleys, but Clohosey's stick got there first, and the leather flashed to the Dublin net for an amazing winning goal.

On the puck-out, referee Kelly of Laois blew the full-time whistle, and the 31,312 crowd were momentarily stunned. Kilkenny followers with delight, Dublin supporters with disappointment.

And the irony of it all was that the man who got the winning goal had, till then, scarcely laid his hurley to the ball.

DUBLIN CONTRIBUTED TO OWN DEFEAT

Said Captain Clohosey in the dressing-room afterwards. 'We were lucky. As for that goal, well I felt I just had to redeem myself. I had given up all hope with 10 minutes to go. I'm truly sorry for luckless Dublin, but still, that's hurling.'

But while, like everyone else who watched the game, I, too, have every sympathy for Dublin, the fact is that they contributed in some measure to their own defeat by falling back too much into defence in the closing stages, and striving to preserve their slender lead rather than seeking to increase it.

This left a gaping hole at midfield, so that every time in the closing stages that the ball was pucked out from the Dublin goal, it was promptly whipped back again by Kilkenny's half-backs or midfielders. Yet, even till that last crashing blow fell, happy Dublin supporters had every reason to believe that their surprising side must win its way to the All-Ireland final for the first time in seven years.

For, though they lacked the finesse of some of the Kilkennymen, the Dubliners made up for any deficiencies by their blood-warming determination, going into every tackle fearlessly and clearing their lines as if they hated the sight of the ball.

BOTH TEAMS RALLIED IN TURN

Hurling as if they had no opposition in the first five minutes, Kilkenny were four points in front before Dublin woke up.

Then the finesse v determination battle started.

First, the Dublin forwards lashed over three points in three minutes; then Tom O'Connell snigged home a neat Kilkenny goal, but the Noremen were a bare point in front at half-time thanks to four great Dublin points by young Des Foley.

Mick Brophy's withdrawal with a head injury midway through the first-half, was a big factor in Dublin's recovery, but Brophy returned on the restart.

Yet Dublin took the lead in the fourth minute of the second-half when Des Foley sent in a long drive which was brought down from over the bar by goalkeeper Ollie Walsh, but he brought it down into his own net. Dublin led 1-8 to 1-6 and from that to the end we saw action-packed hurling.

Foley now moved to midfield where he proceeded to blot out Brophy and, with the Dublin forwards chasing every ball, the metropolitans held a three-point lead with just four minutes left for play.

But Kilkenny never gave up; they fought back for another point and then snatched the honours with that snap goal on the call of time.

WALSHS STARRED IN DEFENCE

The Kilkenny Walshs, Tom, Jim and Mick, never gave a thing away. Martin Treacy made a good debut at centre-half, but Johnny McGovern was not seen at his best until Foley moved off him to midfield.

Midfield exchanges were even over the hour; Paddy Kelly (Kilkenny) and Fran Whelan (Dublin) also having some bright moments there. Mick Fleming and Denis Heaslip were always dangerous in a Kilkenny attack that sadly missed Billy Dwyer, for whom sub goalkeeper Liam Cleere was not an adequate replacement.

Hero of the day as far as Dublin were concerned was little Jimmy Gray in goal. Though beaten in the final seconds, he played a wonderful game, and made some miraculous saves.

Paddy Croke played well at left full-back while the Hayes-Bohane-Malone half-back line was in top form. Des Foley did everything in the attack while there, and got great help from Harry Doyle, Tony Young and Paddy Kenny.

Scorers: Kilkenny – T O'Connell (1-2), S Clohosey (1-0), R Carroll (0-3), M Walsh (0-2), J McGovern (0-1), D Heaslip (0-1); Dublin: D Folely (1-6), H Doyle (0-2), P Kenny (0-2), L Shannon (0-1).

Kilkenny: O Walsh; T Walsh, J Walsh, J Maher; M Walsh, M Treacey, J McGovern; M Brophy, P Kelly; D Heaslip, R Carroll, M Fleming; S Clohosey, L Cleere, T O'Connell. **Subs:** T Kelly for Brophy, Brophy for Kelly, M Kelly for Cleere.

Dublin: J Gray; D Ferguson, B Young, P Croke; C Hayes. M Bohane, E Malone; L Shannon, F Whelan; D Foley, B Boothman, H Doyle; S Dowling, A Young, P Kenny. **Sub:** L Jackson for Dowling.

Referee: E Kelly (Laois).

◄ ◄ ◆ ▷ ▶

1961 LEINSTER HURLING FINAL

by MICK DUNNE

DUBLIN 7-5 WEXFORD 4-8

Tumbling down come champions Wexford and back over the rocky road to Dublin goes the Leinster hurling title. And, in bringing it there after a nine-year absence, Dublin's 'makeshift' forwards proved that they were not so misplaced after all. For in the final at Kilkenny yesterday it was this combination of four defenders, a goalkeeper and a midfielder turned attackers that was primarily responsible for Wexford's dethronement.

Bravely the Dublin selectors gambled; convincingly they scooped in the pool from a game in which there was a rich stake, and, as every card in their hand turned out to be an ace; they had the satisfaction of confounding those who believed they were taking unnecessary risks.

Into an attack already short of recognised hurling forwards they moved two defenders of the top class, Mick Bohan and Paddy Croke, to two key positions. Yet this stop-gap attack proved itself with devastating effectiveness when causing the biggest shock of the hurling year.

Here on Nowlan Park's rich green carpet were six men appearing in what were, in most cases, unaccustomed positions.

But before this tremendously exciting hour of admirably sporting and enjoyable hurling had reached its final moments of great joy for Dublin supporters, these forwards in the sky-blue jerseys played with what seemed a practiced effectiveness and a familiar ease in every position.

When it was all over they had a rich harvest of title-taking scores to show for this smooth moving attack, which outpaced and outsmarted their opponents in most occasions, and used the ball most menacingly in well executed movements that were crowned by a high measure of alert opportunism.

It all amounted to a nightmare hour for an unusually lax Wexford defence in which only Jim English, a wing half-back in a class of his own, can remember the game with any satisfaction.

THIRD QUARTER WAS DECISIVE

These swiftly-moving Dublin forwards forced previously high ranking defenders into unaccustomed blundering and thwarted the best of them for the scores that sent Wexford crashing from their proud pinnacle of championship hurling glory.

Yet, though they showed what they were capable of in the first-half, the metropolitan attackers reserved their greatest and most destructive efforts for the third quarter – the period that utterly shattered Wexford's mounting hopes.

It was Dublin who jumped into a seventh-minute lead when Paddy Croke, full-back in the semi-final and now their full-forward, crashed home a goal.

Fifteen minutes gone and Bernie Boothman, yet another former half-back, stretched that lead when he doubled on a long drive from Des Ferguson, and soon afterwards Croke added another goal that left the comparatively small Dublin following joyously expectant of a long-waited title triumph.

But by the 27th minute that lead had been scrubbed out and goals by Oliver McGrath (two) and Tim Flood, as well as a couple of points left scores all-square. When Flood and Padge Kehoe tacked on points, Wexford led 3-4 to 3-2 at half-time.

Less than four minutes after the restart the alert and busy Tim Flood pounced on the ball when goalkeeper Jim Gray blocked a shot from Padge Kehoe and the Wexford corner forward sank it in the net. Seconds later McGrath added a point that put the champions six points ahead.

DUBLIN'S GREAT FIGHT BACK

Then it seemed that Wexford, having regained their composure after that early and unsettling challenging burst of Dublin's, would demonstrate all the power that made them champions and sweep onto success.

But at that stage we didn't know about that still-unrevealed destruction that lay in the Dublin attack. But, we hadn't to wait long for evidence of it, as Dublin came thundering back with a fighting determination, all the more praiseworthy because it was produced at a time when it looked as though they had lost this Leinster final.

Back they came in surging waves of increasingly threatening attacks that were sparked off by their crisp half-back line and supported by a midfield superiority. And in a six-minute scoring spree they raided with such profitable efficiency that Wexford's crown was toppling with only 13 second-half minutes gone.

It was just after 37 minutes when Larry Shannon sent in a scorching shot that bounced off the wrong side (for Wexford) of the upright and, although full-back Nick O'Donnell got his hand to the rebound and scooped it out, umpire Bob Aylward had no hesitation in flagging a goal that cut the lead to three points.

Mick Bohan quickly added a point and on the 40 minute when goalkeeper Pat Nolan came out to block a shot from Billy Jackson, Paddy Croke rushed in to belt the loose ball into an empty net, and give Dublin back the lead.

Again the Wexford defence was pierced little more than a minute later when Bernie Boothman sent back a rebound from Pat Nolan's save from Shannon's free. It was the 43rd minute when Fran Whelan placed Jackson for Dublin's seventh goal.

So Dublin led 7-3 to 4-6, for, in that six-minute period Wexford could only manage one point which Padge Kehoe hit in the 42nd minute.

Thus Dublin were well on the way to a victory that sends them straight through to the All-Ireland final on September 3 against Tipperary or Cork.

It was their six-pronged attack that started Wexford tottering, but, in the last 10 minutes, it was their magnificently inflexible defence that prevented a courageous Wexford saving their titles.

IT WAS FIERY BUT FAIR

This was a fiery, but always scrupulously fair struggle, a battle for survival in Dublin's case and for the salvation of their title in Wexford that was rare enjoyment for the 27,446 crowd.

None performed with greater credit than goalkeeper Jimmy Gray, who among other daring deeds got his stick to a dangerous shot by Oliver McGrath five minutes from the end. In front of him Gray had a toweringly invincible Noel Drumgoole, a vigilant and a cool full-back who kept such a close watch on Andy Doyle that the Wexford full-forward was not only prevented from repeating his display of the semi-final but was held scoreless.

On Drumgoole's right Des Ferguson waged an exciting battle with Tim Flood and though beaten on occasions, he performed most creditably. But it was the sound half-back line of dashing Liam Ferguson, reliable Christy Hayes and a competent Seán Lynch that took highest honours in curbing the Wexford attack.

Almost every man was back in defence in those last minutes and on one occasion it was the timely intervention of midfielder Des Foley that prevented a certain Wexford goal.

Foley, after a hesitant start, had contributed his share with Fran Whelan in giving Dublin the edge at midfield. He hurled strongly against Ned Wheeler in the first-half and completely blotted out Jim Morrissey in the second. Wheeler, playing almost a lone hand, could never curb this Foley-Whelan superiority.

For Wexford Jim English once again confirmed his greatness as a wing half-back, but on a team that was beaten badly for speed and fitness by a fleet-footed Dublin side he got assistance only from Billy Rackard, Tim Flood and Oliver McGrath.

SCORERS: Dublin – P Croke (3-0), B Boothman (2-0), L Shannon (1-1), W Jackson (1-0), M Bohan (0-2), D Foley (0-1), C Hayes (0-1); **Wexford** – O McGrath (2-2), T Flood (2-2), P Kehoe (0-2), E Wheeler (0-1), J Morrissey (0-1).

Dublin: J Gray; D Ferguson, N Drumgoole, L Foley; L Ferguson, C Hayes, S Lynch; D Foley, F Whelan; A Boothman, M Bohan, L Shannon; B Boothman, P Croke, W Jackson.

Wexford: P Nolan; J Mitchel, N O'Donnell, T Neville; J English, W Rackard, P Wilson; E Wheeler, J Morrissey; J O'Brien, P Kehoe, S Quaid; O McGrath, A

Doyle, T Flood. **Subs:** H Dowdall, for Quaid, M Bergin for A Doyle, A Doyle for Bergin.

Referee – J Dowling (Offaly).

◄◄◄◆▷►

I HAVE BEEN trying to recall what we actually did in the 50s and 60s? All I know is that there is a massive difference between then and now.

We trained twice a week in Parnell Park mainly, and sometimes in O'Toole Park depending on availability. We got socks and knicks for the All-Ireland final. That's all we ever got. Players now are well rigged out at the start of the season, and that is only right. It was a different era and there was no sponsorship of teams.

You had to have your own hurley and, if you broke it, you got a replacement. There was a classic case where Paddy Donnelly turned up with no hurley in Wexford Park one day. Now Paddy really looked after his hurleys… he treated them like classic violins.

The Dublin mentor in charge of hurleys wasn't impressed and he wouldn't give Paddy a hurley, so he went out on the pitch with no hurley. A Wexford selector saw the situation, took pity on him, and gave him one.

Sliotars were very scarce.

We didn't do any warm-ups or drills like they do now. So after a few laps of the field and a few sprints, we would play a 10-a-side match… so you didn't need too many sliotars. There were no formal tactical sessions.

Joe Drumgoole would do most of the talking. Mick Ryan, who was in the army and became a teacher afterwards, was our trainer. Seán McCabe, Jack O'Sullivan from Crumlin, Mick Leahy, Paddy Lillis and Joe were our backroom team.

We would meet at 14 Parnell Square, the Dublin County Board offices.

If playing in Kilkenny, we would have a snack in the Seven Oaks Hotel in Carlow before the game and we would come back for a meal afterwards. In fairness, we were well looked after in that department. But we didn't have a physio or a first aid person.

One of the selectors would do the needful with the magic bottle and sponge.

DES FOLEY WAS, as I've stated, our leader on the pitch. He could strike from both sides and he covered lots of ground during a game. But Achill Boothman was an artist with the hurley and had pace and speed to match. He could run for a week.

Very few backs liked having the job of marking him. Larry Shannon and Christy Hayes were excellent. Noel Drumgoole was a superb full-back and you felt safe behind him. Snitchy Ferguson was a great corner-back with great anticipation and was always in the right place. He always made good use of the ball and looked to find a teammate. Lar Foley wouldn't be regarded as a stylist but he was very strong and fearless.

We would normally spend 10-to-15 minutes playing ground hurling only. But often in a game, the ground ball wouldn't go very far as the grass was too long and, sometimes, the ball was heavy due to the rain. We didn't really practice any other specific skills such as overhead hurling.

Wexford introduced catching the ball, so some teams worked on overhead pulling just to counteract that. Snitchy Ferguson had a wonderful knack of catching balls even when marking taller men. We sometimes trained in the Army Grounds in the Phoenix Park and there was this old lad who was always there watching us.

One night, he spoke with us. 'In my day we played overhead hurling all the time,' he told us. 'The ball would go from player to player with an overhead shot and it would eventually reach the full-forward line not having touched the ground. I was playing one night and it was getting a bit dullish and when the sliotar reached me, I pulled and I hit a blackbird.'

Overhead hurling is now a forgotten skill.

I am not a fan of short passing. It has a place when getting rid of a ball when under pressure but I can't take this passing for the sake of passing… so often it breaks down after a few passes. I find it hard to understand the short-game plan because, as the backs dilly dally with the ball, the poor forwards are being starved of quick ball… and any forward worth his salt will tell you he prefers the quick ball.

The short puckout totally frustrates me, as it often breaks down so near the defender's goal. Dublin have conceded a fair few scores in the past few years because of this tactic and I know it drives the supporters mad. I have seen goalies hit a short puck-out straight to an opponent, who taps it over the bar.

I understand the theory that possession is nine-tenths of the law and the longer we hold on to the ball the better. But, my issue is that the longer we hold on to it, the greater chance it will breakdown. I believe you should get the ball to the other end of the field in as fast a manner as possible.

I don't like the rucks.

Players are much more mobile now than in my time. Nowadays, it is not unusual to see a defender up in the attack and indeed to see a forward back helping out the defence. Corner-backs in my time stayed in their own area and hence you wouldn't have more than two players on the ball and therefore rucks were not a feature then.

A lot of players wouldn't have the fitness to stray away from their zone. In the modern game, with the emphasis on possession, when a player runs to the ball, rather than hitting it first time, he tries to rise it and is immediately challenged by a few more players… and the ball ends up on the ground as nobody is able to control it.

I cannot believe that the modern coaches are not encouraging their players to tip the ball out to the side and avoid this awful pile-up of players. It looks terrible and does nothing for the game. There should only be two players in the ruck and whoever has possession of the ball should move it out to the side.

The reason that there were no rucks in my time was because players moved the ball on the ground and didn't try to rise it at every occasion. I watched three hurling games recently and didn't see one example of two players going shoulder-to-shoulder, pulling on the ball.

I would have to admit that hurling in my time was much dirtier than now.

The tactics in those days often zoned in on dealing with one or two stars on the opposing team. That meant taking them out of the game by any means, foul or fair.

Fr Tommy Maher played a major part in changing that attitude. Kilkenny had one or two boyos, but generally they concentrated on hurling and they excelled at winning the ball and then getting it away to another player. For that reason, I liked playing Kilkenny even though we didn't win too often.

With a few other teams, you were taking your life in your hands. I remember down in Clare one day in horrendous conditions and the muck in the goal area was dreadful. There was a schemozzle and players were pulling away and not too concerned where the ball was. Lar Foley deliberately stood on the ball... and it was lost in the muck.

This didn't stop the wayward pulling. The referee came in and said, 'Lads, there is no ball there so take it easy!'

And Lar replied, 'That's how they play it down here ref!'

One day my father went to a match in Islandbridge and he got into a row. We were playing Kickhams. They had a guy from Tipperary playing midfield and he gave me a dirty belt. Vinny Bell came in and clocked the Tipperary man who hit me.

My dad was in the middle of it. The strategy of the time was don't take any prisoners and get your retaliation in first. Hurling was very dirty in those days and you could be in jail today for some of the things that happened then.

I like many facets of the modern game and the way it is played. The basis of hurling is skill and that was not always the way. Players today are so skilful and they are a joy to watch. I enjoy watching teams during the puckaround before the start of a game.

Their skill level is extraordinary and that comes obviously from good coaching and lots of practice. Even when kids come on the pitch at half-time I enjoy watching them and their skill level is definitely better than some players in my time.

It is often levelled at the modern game that ground hurling is a forgotten art. People say that hurling in my time was all about ground hurling. I wouldn't agree with that. Actually, some players back then struggled with lifting the ball when running at full speed and that is why they pulled on the ball. Some players wouldn't be happy taking a free or a sideline cut.

The full-back line didn't need too much skill, as their main function was to keep the man out and let the ball into the goalie. Mick Maher, the Tipperary full-back on the 60s told the story that at the final whistle in one All-Ireland, Tommy Barrett, the Tipperary secretary, came on the field to congratulate the players.

'Well done, you had a great game,' he said to Mick.

'Well, if I had,' says Mick, 'I didn't touch the ball once!'

Hurling now is a better game because of the high skill level and that is acknowledged by all. I must say though that I miss the clash of the ash – two players running at speed and then pulling as hard as they can. It was a feature in my days and that always added spice to the game. You rarely see that now.

You seldom see hurleys broken during games now. In the good old days a lot of hurleys were broken when players doubled on the overhead ball, or when two players were shoulder-to-shoulder and pulled on the ball.

THE ROLE OF the goalkeeper is a bit easier today than in my time.

The full-forward line, as well as scoring, took great pleasure in intimidating the poor old goalie and if possible putting him in the back of the net. Tony Young was a top class hurler for us. He could play in any position on the pitch. He was a tough man and when we played Kilkenny, Tony was picked at full-forward with the purpose of getting in and frightening the great Ollie Walsh.

In the 1961 team, Paddy Croke, who was a defender really, was put up in the full-forward line to throw his weight about and cause confusion among the opposition. The high ball coming into the square was a chance for the forwards to rush the goalie and make him take his eye off the ball.

You depended on your full-back line to protect you.

I was lucky with my three full-backs and I was rarely upended in the goalmouth. It happened me once in Cork when Christy Ring got through our full-back line and I found myself in the net.

I met him socially years later and he reminded me of the incident. Mickey the 'Rattler' Byrne, Mick Maher, John Doyle and Kieran Carey took no messing around the square and you took your life in your hands if you dared approach that goalmouth. Doyle is reported as saying to his full-back line partners, after a nippy corner-forward got through for a score… 'Lads, lower the bar!'

I DON'T LIKE the 'sweeper' idea.

Scoring is difficult enough when it's six defenders versus six forwards. By having a 'sweeper' you have reduced your goal chances as you now have only five forwards marking six backs, and possibly seven backs if the opponents play a similar system. The number of goals scored is now less than formerly but that is compensated by the number of excellent points scored from all over the field.

Joe Canning was a joy to watch, whether from play, a free or a sideline cut. But I am slightly concerned when a player can score sometimes up to 16 points… lads like TJ. Reid, Aaron Gillane, Patrick Horgan, Donal Burke, Lee Chin… Tony

Kelly and many more are excellent free-takers. What would happen, I wonder, if the player who is fouled had to take the free? Not many players would like having to take a crucial free that would decide who wins the game. It might also reduce the number of frees.

I DO NOT agree with the black card plan. There isn't the same cynicism in hurling as in football and it will be very difficult for referees to implement it fairly.

The referees were no better or worse in our time than they are now.

The big difference is that the referees now are much fitter and they get good feed-back from the referee assessors.

The role of the team manager is very important. I know, some of them are very big into media exposure, but if they do their job properly they justify their existence. One time, most inter-county teams had five selectors and often they were giving mixed messages to the players. One voice is necessary and I learned that from watching Kevin Heffernan in action.

The backroom team has grown and grown and I think that is a good idea, provided the number is manageable. I read that one inter-county team has 24 backroom staff. This seems to me to be excessive and probably very costly as well.

THE SPLIT-SEASON seems to be the way forward. The clubs are now getting a better deal than formerly. They can play their league games during the inter-county season and then welcome back their players for the club championship. Players should be guaranteed a minimum of 20 games a year.

We have a great system in Dublin where we have an excellent league that is taken very seriously by all clubs. That is followed by a round robin championship, and cup matches are played at different times during the season.

I still enjoy watching hurling games at all levels. Saturday morning in my own club, watching the nursery, is a joy to behold. Obviously, the lockdowns put a damper on that for a while. Our juvenile section run thousands of games per year and the standard of hurling in the past 20 years has improved a hundred fold.

I AM CONCERNED about player welfare. Some very talented young players are expected to train with five or six teams. The danger is that they will be burned out and lose interest in playing and actually give it up.

Clubs do need to have a welfare officer who makes the final call on how many sessions and games a player can attend in a week. Some managers are only interested in their own team and don't see the bigger picture.

Obviously, I would love to see Dublin winning an All-Ireland senior title. We nearly did it in 1961 and again in 2013. But, whether we do or we don't, the great satisfaction for me is in the increase in the number playing hurling, and camogie today.

Long may it be so.

I HAVE LOVED watching Dublin hurling matches in the last decade more than ever before, to be honest. I have great memories, of great games, and great trips with friends.

We were lucky to have Anthony Daly as our manager for a good few years!

Daly was a wonderful manager. He lifted the morale in the county and the players responded. He was so unlucky not to have won an All-Ireland in his time with Dublin. The 2011 National League final win over Kilkenny was magnificent and, then me being given the honour of presenting the Leinster Championship trophy to Dublin captain Johnny McCaffrey in 2013 was beyond my wildest dreams.

As the year wore on and on in the 2011 season, I had a good feeling about our team. I saw progress in almost every game. More and more players were putting their names on certain jerseys and there was no great turnover of players during the league.

The main reason for that was the fact that more matches were won rather than lost.

We drew with Waterford away and at home to Kilkenny. Leaving Parnell Park that day I felt we could have an unusually good season. It is always special to be able to stay with Kilkenny. We defeated Tipperary, Wexford and Offaly. The only loss was to Galway.

For our last league game, we were away to Cork. Meanwhile, Waterford were at home to Galway. Waterford and Dublin were fighting for runners-up spot and a straight run into the final.

We were leading narrowly as the minutes ticked away and, at the same time, Waterford were just ahead of Galway. I always remember Dublin switching captain Johnny McCaffrey to right half-back as Cork were doing a lot of dangerous attacking from that wing. Johnny stopped the supply of ball into the Cork full-forward line and Dublin ran out to win by a point… 1-15 to 1-14. Even though Waterford won also, we just pipped them on score difference. We had a wonderful trip back on the FODH (Friends of Dublin Hurling) bus that evening.

We knew we were facing Kilkenny in the final but we had a bit of confidence after the drawn game in Parnell Park.

The running joke for years during the 90s and after was that the Kilkenny B team was the second best team in Leinster. While they were short a few players for the final, we knew that any player who puts on a Kilkenny shirt in a final is well capable of playing a blinder and winning the game for his team. So we were prepared for a very tough game, but hoping for a win.

Dublin hadn't won a league final in 72 years.

Very few outsiders gave us any chance and most expected The Cats to put the Dubs to the sword. As it worked out, it was the exact opposite. Dublin had a comprehensive 12-point win and kept Kilkenny's score to 1-7. It is a very long time since Kilkenny had such a low score. We had the aid of a fairly strong wind in the first-half, so it was vital to have a respectable lead going into half-time.

Eddie Brennan got a good goal for the cats in the 10th minute and we said, 'Here we go again!' But in actual fact it was the Dubs who got going and they had eight unanswered points to leave the half-time score at 0-11 to 1-2.

The big question at half-time was… would six points be sufficient now having to face the wind? Maurice O'Brien, who had come on as a sub, started the scoring in the second-half with a long distance point. TJ Reid scored a few points for Kilkenny from frees but, for once, he was unusually off target with his frees and had a few poor wides.

IT WAS A long time since I had the privilege of going to Croke Park in the month of August to watch my own county playing in an All-Ireland hurling semi-final. There was no great pressure on Dublin, in 2011, as Tipp were raging favourites, especially after their annihilation of Waterford in the Munster final by seven goals.

Dublin already had their best year in a long time in winning the league final by giving Kilkenny a hiding, although The Cats got their revenge two months later in the Leinster final. Dublin recovered from that defeat and headed for Thurles to take on Limerick in the All-Ireland quarter-final.

There was a great buzz on the Friends of Dublin Hurling bus as this was new territory for us. We beat Limerick, with Ryan O'Dwyer getting three goals in a 10-minute period. It was a massive win for Dublin and we were already looking forward to the semi-final. As we were approaching our bus for the journey home, I was surprised to see four Dublin fans on their bicycles heading for the square.

Surely, they hadn't cycled all the way from Dublin, like in the old days.

No, they had travelled by car from Dublin as far as Two-Mile Borris and then cycled the eight kilometres to Semple Stadium. The four lads – great O'Toole's members – Des O'Brien and his youngest son Daragh, Brendan Plunkett and Eamon Ryan, decided to cycle part of the way so as to avoid congestion and, of course, to get their daily exercise.

They were in great form and were heading to Liberty Square for 'tae and sangers'. They were over the moon with the Dublin performance.

Anthony Daly had his homework done and decided to devise tactics to stem the flow of ball into their full-forward line, but we had the worst possible start in the third minute when a fumble led to Lar Corbett tapping the ball into the net. This would rattle any team but the Dubs dug deep and over the following 17 minutes they outscored Tipp by nine points to three.

They were giving a massive fright to the Tipp boys.

Tipp came back with a few scores before Gary Maguire made a wonderful save to prevent what looked like a certain goal. Peter Kelly, after a shaky start, had a wonderful game... high catching and bursting out of defence. He finished off one raid with a long distance point – not bad for a full-back. While we weren't as efficient in the second-half, Tipp still failed to shake us off and they needed a few late points to make sure of victory.

◄ ◄ ◆ ► ►

THEY ALWAYS SAY you never give a second chance to teams like Kilkenny.

That was the fear in 2013... in the Leinster Championship semi-final. We probably should have won the first day. Kilkenny got the equalising point with the last puck of the game from TJ Reid. So we headed for O'Moore Park in Portlaoise on a beautiful Saturday evening for the replay.

On the bus, I must say there was a great buzz on the way down. I really enjoy travelling on the FODH bus as it is great value and you meet fellow Dublin fans. There were three packed buses that famous evening.

Thousands travelled by car, obviously, and the atmosphere in the ground was electric. I met a few Kilkenny fans who told me that we had missed the boat. I have many great friends in Kilkenny but some of them can be heavy going when you are playing them.

They expect to win every game… and maybe that is why they win so much. I must admit I wasn't impressed at the drawn game when I heard a few Kilkenny supporters bad mouthing Brian Cody.

The replay started at fever pitch and Dublin were first out of the blocks. Dotsy O'Callaghan was in superb form and he caused lots of problems for Jackie Tyrrell. Dotsy has a wonderful sidestep and feint, and he scored four beautiful points on the night. By half-time we were four points in front. While four points is a nice lead it is never enough when playing the top team in the country. Kilkenny came out in the second-half and they cut the lead to two points and I was fearing for the worst at that stage.

But we kept tagging on the points. Liam Rushe was outstanding at centre half-back. Midway in the second-half Dotsy O'Callaghan won possession, rounded a few Kilkenny defenders and had his shot stopped on the line and cleared to Danny Sutcliffe, who pulled first time to the back of the net.

It was a wonderful goal and I must say I felt we had a chance of making history as all our players were on top of their game. Kilkenny are never defeated, but the Dublin defence was outstanding and closed down their forwards. With time running out and only three points in the difference, Kilkenny got a free 50 yards out and Eoin Larkin lobbed it into the square.

Colin Fennelly won possession and started to charge his way into the parallelogram but he had five Dublin defenders to pass. So often in moments like this the referee gives a free in to the attacker. But to our great delight, Barry Kelly blew his whistle for a free out and the game ended there.

I was numb at that stage and it took me a while to get my bearings. It was 42 years since we had beaten Kilkenny in a championship game. The Dublin fans ran on to the pitch and the players remained there for a long time to celebrate with their loyal supporters.

Anthony Daly and his management team had a wonderful night on the line.

We enjoyed our trip back home on the bus. So often in the past we came home with our tail between our legs after another defeat. This was a special night and we celebrated. After it had sunk in, then we started thinking about the Leinster final against Galway.

What a great night to be a Dublin hurling supporter.

NOW THAT WE had beaten Kilkenny, we had to face Galway, who were the holders of the Bob O'Keeffe Cup. It was a long way back to 1961, when Dublin last won it and I had the pleasure of being in goal for the Dubs.

This would be our fifth game in as many weeks and while people talk about player burnout, I felt our team was getting better by the week and were enjoying playing matches back-to-back.

Again, it was another beautiful day in early July.

I had attended games in Croke Park for about 70 years but this day was so special because Dublin were in a Leinster hurling final and had a real chance of being crowned champions. When I reached Croke Park I was so delighted to see Hill 16 filling up nicely.

It was a great boost for the players to have the Hill on their side.

Joe Canning scored the first point from a free, but then Dublin got going and by midway in the first-half were leading by five points. Paul Ryan was tapping over the points and Dotsy O'Callaghan continued where he left off the previous game. He won a ball and rounded Fergal Moore and, when everybody thought he would shoot, he turned back and passed the ball to Paul Ryan who cracked it into the net.

We went in leading 1-12 to 0-7. Speaking to a few Dubs during the half-time cup of tea, I felt there was an expectation that Dublin could win this.

I was quietly confident, but I know that an eight-point lead isn't that great in a hurling game. Also, I was aware that Joe Canning could turn it on at any moment.

Five minutes into the second-half and Paul Ryan got his second goal. Conal Keaney fielded a high ball and sent it in to Paul, who rattled the net… a rasper. Yes, we were feeling very confident now. However, Galway had other ideas and they scored two goals in the space of five minutes.

Gary Maguire made two wonderful saves then from Joe Canning and David Burke, and that settled Dublin. At this stage my heart was in my mouth.

Mark Schutte won a great ball but finished poorly when a goal was on. Conor McCormack and Danny Sutcliffe added points to push the lead out to eight points. We looked the fresher team on the day and finished strongly… a big win.

So eight days after beating Kilkenny in a classic, we repeated the performance and claimed the Bob O'Keeffe Cup. Another great performance by the players, and Anthony Daly and his backroom team. Savouring the win, I gave my thanks to John Costello and the county board for their wise choice in opting for Daly in 2009.

It paid huge dividends for hurling in general.

THE SEMI-FINAL WAS a wonderful game of hurling.

The game had *everything* – a beautiful sunny day, over 62,000 people watching, teams level 15 times during the 70 minutes, 18 scorers… and fantastic shooting from both sets of forwards. The pace of the game was staggering and the ball control was top drawer stuff.

Referees play such an important role and James Owens had a good game overall, but I must dispute his decision to send off Ryan O'Dwyer.

Ryan got a yellow card in the second minute of the first-half. The incident happened near the sideline under the Hogan Stand. I have watched it many times since and still feel it was very harsh. In the modern game, managers are concerned when a player gets a yellow as he has to be extra careful for the remainder of the game.

In the 51st minute Ryan had a clumsy tackle on a Cork defender and got a second yellow. Most analysts agreed that the second yellow was warranted, but that the first one was too harsh. That is my understanding as well. Obviously, the referee has a difficult job and mistakes will be made but it is maddening when you are at the wrong end of it.

Dublin had to play the last 20 minutes with 14 men.

To add insult to injury, the Cork goalie Anthony Nash took the resultant free from roughly 100 yards out and sent it sailing over the bar. Psychologically, this was a key moment for Cork. But fair play to the Dubs, they dug deep.

It is very hard to enjoy a game when your own team is involved, but I must admit I could only admire the skill and commitment of both teams. The scores came thick and fast and we were treated to some fantastic point scoring. Danny

Sutcliffe, Conal Keaney, Dotsy O'Callaghan and Paul Ryan got some wonderful scores. Anthony Nash scored three long distance points and had a wonderful save from a rocket from Ryan O'Dwyer when a Dublin goal would have been a massive boost.

Both teams were excellent in finding their men. David Treacy's goal was a wonderful team goal and again full marks to the coaches involved.

The Cork goal wasn't as classy. Gary Maguire came out to gather the ball, and as the ball was on to way into his hand, Pat Horgan intercepted it and tapped it into the net. A good goal for them but a disaster for us. Cork were only a point up before they got the goal. So, Dublin had battled on with 14 men for 20 minutes and the game never looked over until that goal went in.

Do I think Dublin would have won if they had a full team?

Yes, I do. And I also think they would have beaten Clare in the final. It would have been a dream to have won it, 75 years after Dublin's last All-Ireland win in 1938.

◄◄◆►►

2018 WAS THE year the round robin system was introduced.

It was a long time in coming. It was so disheartening for teams like Dublin to have only one championship game during the summer months. It is amazing how the powers-that-be didn't see the need to give more championship games to the weaker counties.

The league provided five or six games but they were played in winter conditions normally. In the 70s and 80s the league usually started in October, and finished in April. Teams didn't train during the winter months in those days.

Still, the games were good as all teams were at the same level of fitness. Dublin had the bad luck of drawing Kilkenny in the first round of the championship too often, and of course losing to them. So before the summer had really arrived, the championship was over for Dublin and some of the weaker counties. Galway, on the other hand, didn't have a provincial championship, and they could start training in June for their first game in late-July.

Looking back on it now, you would have to ask the question why wasn't the situation rectified years earlier.

So, it was wonderful to be looking forward to having four Leinster Championship games in the space of five weeks. It was broadly welcomed by all hurling people. Dublin's first game in the series was a home game to Kilkenny.

There was a big build-up and it was an all-ticket affair. Pat Gilroy had taken over from Ger Cunningham as manager and there was a sense of expectancy around. Pat had proved himself with the footballers and he brought a successful management team with him, one of whom was the great Mickey Whelan, who was my trainer when I managed the senior hurlers in the early-90s.

I got the impression from watching league games that Dublin were returning to a more direct style of hurling – get the ball into the other team's square as quickly as possible.

The game started in a welter of excitement and it was obvious that Dublin were up for the challenge. The tackling was ferocious and a lot of man-to-man marking. Dublin had Eoghan O'Donnell marking Kilkenny's most dangerous player, TJ Reid. Eoghan had a powerful game and held TJ to one point from play. Dublin had Liam Rushe at full-forward and he caused serious problems for the Kilkenny defence.

What really impressed me was that Liam got a good supply of balls from the half-backs and midfielders, and Padraig Walsh struggled to contain him.

Even though he didn't score, he was the cause of the three goals, winning possession and laying the ball off to Paul Ryan, Fergal Whitely and Jake Malone... and they did the rest. Conal Keaney was getting the upper-hand on Cillian Buckley and he was a constant thorn for the Kilkenny defenders.

The Kilkenny goal only came in the last few minutes and in my humble opinion, it should have been a free out as Paddy Smyth was fouled in possession of the ball.

That goal put Kilkenny in the lead, which Dublin had for all but the first four minutes of the game. It was a sickening blow for a team that had worked so hard. The Dublin crowd, most of whom were on the terraces, were stunned and silenced.

The majority of the patrons in the stand were Kilkenny supporters as they had the season tickets and were thereby guaranteed a seat.

Putting the disappointment aside, it was another wonderful game of hurling and it was great to see a packed Parnell Park on a beautiful day in May.

◄ ◄ ◆ ► ►

IT SEEMS AGES ago since we witnessed Dublin's wonderful game against Galway, in the championship in Parnell Park, in 2019.

Parnell Park hasn't seen enough of games like that one.

The sun was shining on a beautiful Saturday evening in June. This was the final game of the round robin series and there was lots of discussion on the various possible results and their implications. The other big game that evening was Wexford hosting Kilkenny in Wexford Park. For Dublin to progress to the Leinster final, we had to beat Galway and there had to be a winner in Wexford.

Parnell Park was packed again for a hurling game.

Kids everywhere with hurleys in their hands. All the hard work in Dublin to promote hurling was paying off and the increase in the number of young kids playing the game is a joy to behold. Many thanks to the clubs, Cumann na mBunscol and the Parnell Park staff.

Dublin were short our two main free-takers, Paul Ryan and David Treacy, and that was a big concern as free-takers can win and lose games. On the night, Oisín O'Rourke stepped up and had a wonderful game, scoring nine points. He may not be the biggest player on the pitch but he is a nightmare for defenders, and his first touch and speed is top class.

Galway's main concern was would Joe Canning be fit enough to make an appearance at some stage. As it happened, he did come on midway in the second-half and we feared for the worst as Joe is so dangerous around goal.

He scored two points but thankfully he didn't get near enough to goal and the Dublin defence were on their best behaviour and didn't give away any close-in frees.

The first-half was keenly contested. Galway had a slight advantage for most of the half. But Dublin came alive when Eamon Dillon got a cheeky goal. It was a pity Galway replied with four points in-a-row to go in leading by one point at half-time.

Dublin had a great second-half start. Chris Crummey carried the ball up field and evaded a few tackles before being brought down by a Galway defender. Another defender, Seán Moran, stepped up and he hit the back of the net with the penalty. Conal Keaney took the lead for Dublin. He was immense at centre half-forward and gave a torrid time to his marker Joseph Cooney. He caught some spectacular overhead balls, gave some accurate passes to better placed teammates and scored three points himself.

At his best there isn't a better centre half-forward in Ireland. Chris Crummey wasn't far behind him. He played a captain's part and led by example. When the game was on a knife-edge with time running out, he came forward again and scored a wonderful goal to make victory nearly secure. Danny Sutcliffe scored the final point to put the game beyond Galway's reach.

The scenes after the game brought tears to my eyes.

The Dublin supporters ran on to the pitch to congratulate their heroes. A lot of people had their phones to their ears as the game in Wexford Park was still in play. Galway players were standing still waiting for the result. Their worst fears were realised when the other game ended in a draw. Galway were out of the 2019 championship.

I felt sorry for them as they were a serious team and could have won the All-Ireland if they got another chance. Dublin would have preferred a different result from Wexford as they would have made the Leinster final if Wexford or Kilkenny had lost. However, the consolation was a place in the All-Ireland quarter final.

Another great occasion and I was glad to have witnessed it.

The game of hurling has certainly changed since Jimmy Gray's playing days. Here he fields (right) a ball in a cluster of players during the 1961 All-Ireland hurling final while (below) Lar Foley and Dublin selector Joe Drumgoole and Dublin captain Noel Drumgoole remonstrate with referee Gerry Fitzgerald after Foley was sent off in the same game.

« CHAPTER 14 »

More to Life

CON COTTRELL, A Cork hurler, was running the Blind School in Drumcondra. He succeeded in getting an 'appeal' slot on radio and he asked Christy Ring if he would do it for him. Christy agreed, and Con asked me to come along as we knew each other.

Christy made a very good appeal.

Afterwards, we were chatting and he said to me, 'What are you doing now that you are retired?'

'I'm playing a bit of golf,' I said.

Christy came back, 'How good are you?'

'Mediocre,' I said.

'The same as your hurling!' was Christy's reply.

Dublin played the Rest of Ireland in a charity game for St Vincent's on the Navan Road. At the after the match meal the local priest said a few words and it was very obvious he didn't know much about hurling. The nun in charge, a Cork woman, asked me if I would ask Christy to speak on behalf the teams.

He said a lovely few words and finished with, 'Father, you keep saying the Masses and we will do the hurling!'

Ring had a great sense of humour, but he rarely smiled when he told jokes.

THERE IS NO need for four Provincial Councils.

In Leinster you have 24 people coming to a meeting and making fixtures, that could easily have been made in Croke Park. I mentioned to John Horan that he should look at that when he became president. I met him subsequently and asked if they made any progress?

'Jimmy, it's a no-go area!' he replied. 'Munster will say, What about the Munster Final?'

The other provinces will have reasons of their own why they should be there. It's a total waste of money.

Ireland is too small for four different provincial committees. I know that I will not be popular for saying this, but I really believe it.

We are all reluctant to change, but sometimes change is necessary in order to move with the times. For example, for years people had been asking for more time to be given to clubs. It had gone to the stage where competitions like the O'Byrne Cup and the Walsh Cup were starting in December.

Then Covid came on the scene, and we were forced to make changes.

One of the big changes is the split season, where clubs get five months to run their games with all their county players. And now everybody is saying that it is a great idea. It's a win-win situation for everybody.

The county boards are only paying expenses for five or six months for the county teams. And the clubs are having all their players for five or six months. This would never have happened only for Covid.

My only concern is for the county player… as he or she will be going for the full year.

I'M OFTEN ASKED the question… Would Dublin hurling have prospered like Dublin football if Kevin Heffernan was the Dublin hurling manager?

My answer is always 'Yes!'

Kevin was a great club hurler and I am convinced, as already explained, that if we had him in 1961 we would have won the All-Ireland. He had a great hurling brain as well as a great football brain, and I have no doubt that he would have done wonders with the hurlers. However, it was not to be

KEVIN MORAN WAS a wonderful player, and he came from a wonderful family. They moved to Walkinstown in the late-60s and they bought the Kokonut shop. I would often call in to see Kevin's mother.

She was a lovely lady and she would say to me, 'Jimmy Gray, what are the two most important things in life?' And before I had a chance to answer, she would say, 'Health and education'. Then she would add, 'And where are the cuts made by the government at the moment?' Again, she would not wait for my answer but would say, 'Health and education'.

Kevin's brother Brendan, who died in the recent past, was chairman of Ballyboden St Enda's. He would often call me up for a chat and advice on some problem that he would have in the club.

Kevin, of course, joined Manchester United and became a top class defender.

Alex Ferguson, the manager, when he came into the club, found a drinking culture and he decided to let some of the players go... and that included Kevin. Now Kevin was not a drinker as such, but he enjoyed the company of some of those guys like Norman Whiteside, Paul McGrath and Bryan Robson.

Ferguson, in later years, said that one of his greatest mistakes was letting Kevin go.

DUAL PLAYING SHOULD be avoided where possible.

Some of the smaller clubs may have no choice but to play dual players. Obviously, at underage it is okay as some players are not sure what game they prefer. With all the training and coaching going on now, dual players are suffering from burnout at a very early stage and sometimes they give up both games.

It is not physically possible to give of your best to two sports that are so different. Dublin have had more than their share of dual players, like Kevin Heffernan, Snitchy Ferguson, Des Foley, Lar Foley, Eugene Davey, Mick Holden, Liam Walsh, Shane Ryan, David Henry, Conal Keaney, Dermot Connolly, Dotsy O'Callaghan, Ciarán Kilkenny, Cormac Costello, Con O'Callaghan... just to mention a few.

Hurling has lost some great hurlers to football during that time. In some cases, the players were better footballers and did well. In other cases, players went from hurling to football and spent most of the time on the subs bench.

I BROUGHT DOUGLAS Finlayson, a Scottish friend of mine who worked in the shipping business, to a Leinster final in Croke Park. He was highly impressed by the whole spectacle and during a conversation later on he told me he was a big fan of the game of shinty, which was mainly played in the Highlands of Scotland.

He invited me to visit Scotland to check it out.

A few months later, I met Pat Leahy of the Oliver Plunkett's club and he told me that his club had hosted a under-15 shinty team from Scotland. He gave me a name of a journalist in Oban who was a great shinty fan. So, as I was due to go to Scotland on business, I decided to contact the journalist, George Slater.

George gave me a guided tour of the Highlands and we went to a game in Inverness. I was suitably impressed and was of the opinion that there was potential in maybe having an international between our two countries. When I got home, I dropped a line to president Pat Fanning. Pat was enthusiastic about the idea and himself, Jimmy Smyth and myself went over to Inverness to a shinty cup final and we met the top men in the Camanacht Association, John Campbell, Douglas McIntosh and Jack Redmond.

Some compromised rules were agreed upon and, in 1972, a top class team from Ireland went to Inverness and won a game on the score of 6-4 to 4-5. One of the rules was that you could not catch the ball... and I felt that Tony Doran would struggle with that rule. I was mistaken, as Tony had a blinder and scored goals from the ground with ease. He was an outstanding hurler.

The international series continues now and the players seem to enjoy it very much.

Some clubs from both countries visit each other and enjoy the game and the social interaction as well. My own club Na Fianna were one of the first clubs to invite over a senior team. We used to have a great weekend that finished up with a ceili on the Sunday night.

To this day, some Camanacht people come over for our big games every year and frequently end up in our club during the night.

I HAD BEEN going to Croke Park on St Patrick's Day for about 80 years.

The Railway Cup finals were the highlights for many people all over Ireland on the feast day of our national saint. Crowds of 60,000 attended these games and we witnessed some wonderful performances of hurling and football. Christy Ring, Nickey Rackard, Mick Mackey... these men were a big attraction for many years and they drew large crowds.

In the 50s when I was playing for Dublin, I had the privilege of wearing the Leinster jersey as sub goalie to the great Ollie Walsh. He was an outstanding goalie and I was honoured to be named as his No 2. It was great to have the privilege of playing with the stars from other counties. We mixed well and always loved to beat Munster, who regarded themselves as the best.

In due time, the Railway Cup just faded away. The crowds fell to the hundreds and on one occasion at a semi-final it is reckoned there were less that 100 people in attendance.

The club championships were introduced in 1971 and they took over from the Railway Cups. The crowds have grown almost every year and it has been wonderful to see clubs from all over Ireland having the opportunity to display their skills in Croke Park. I have enjoyed all the games and the excitement of supporters, who in some cases were paying their first visit to the sacred sod of Croke Park.

Fourteen Dublin football teams graced the Croke Park sod on St Patrick's Day, winning eight titles. It has been a different story with the game of hurling.

Cuala are the only Dublin club to contest an All-Ireland senior hurling club final. In 2017 they had a win over Tony Kelly-led Ballyea. It was a great joy to see Cuala's captain Oisín Gough climbing the steps to receive the Tommy Moore Cup. And they repeated the success the following year with a win over Na Piarsaigh in a replay in Portlaoise.

These two wins were a great boost to hurling in Dublin, as the Dublin senior hurlers had won a National League and a Leinster title in the previous few years.

PEOPLE TALK ABOUT brand names.

Very few companies, if any, are as famous and as well-known as Cumann na mBunscol. I started my hurling in their leagues back in the 30s and 40s. The teachers who give up of their own time to train and manage teams are so well regarded in schools and clubs. So often, when a player wins an All-Ireland in Croke Park, he will pay tribute to his teachers in primary school who gave him a love of hurling and football.

We, at Friends of Dublin Hurling, really appreciate the work that the Cumann na mBunscol teachers do in promoting hurling and football in Dublin schools. In 2010 we honoured Fintan Walsh with the Lar Foley Hall of Fame Award.

Fintan was a school principal, a member of Ballyboden St Enda's and a massive enthusiast for hurling. In 2019, we honoured Gerry Grogan. Gerry, a Kerryman, has been the voice of Cumann na mBunscol for many years and only retired recently. He is also the voice of the GAA at all big games in Croke Park.

In 2018, Cumann na mBunscol were celebrating 80 years of service to the youth of Dublin. We honoured the schools of the founder members.

From the very beginning, Cumann na mBunscol officers decided that the period from Christmas to summer every year would be dedicated to hurling. The exponential growth from eight schools to nearly 500 has been quite phenomenal. The traditional Dublin clubs grew from the local primary schools and all the great Dublin hurlers – like the Foley brothers, Achill Boothman, Billie Jackson – played in Cumann na mBunscol leagues and finals.

Practically all players who have represented Dublin over the years are Cumann na mBunscol graduates and many of the current hurling and football panels played and captained their schools in Croke Park. Footballers Cian O'Sullivan, Philly McMahon and Cormac Costello were all hurling captains. All Star Liam Rushe led Coláiste Phádraig, in Lucan, to Croke Park success.

Dave Hanley, a Waterford native and teacher in Whitefriar St, was a major driver of hurling development in the early years. He was the first president of Cumann na mBunscol and chairman from 1930 to '33. At a time when sponsorship was difficult to secure, he started a relationship with the *Evening Herald* which is still valued. The *Herald* supplied hurleys to needy schools and presented the Herald Cup – the blue riband of Division 1 Cumann na mBunscol hurling. 2018 marked the 80th anniversary of Corn Herald.

Dave Hanley was a man of many parts. He commentated on several hurling games on Radio Éireann, including the 1938 All-Ireland hurling final after which Mícheál Ó Hehir began his broadcasting career. This was the last time Dublin won the MacCarthy Cup. As we celebrate 90 years of Cumann na mBunscol, we remember the pioneering efforts of the great teachers from the eight founding schools who gathered together in 100 Seville Place, headquarters of O'Toole's GAA Club in 1928.

They sowed the seeds of the current thriving hurling scene in the capital. Another visit from Liam MacCarthy to city schools would be a fitting tribute to these men and a major boost for further promotion and development of our ancient game.

IN THE YEAR 2000 John Bailey, the Dublin chairman, set up a review group to look at all aspects of Dublin hurling and to draw up a list of recommendations that would enable Dublin to become a stronger hurling county. The committee members were Michael O'Grady, Humphrey Kelleher, Mick Dempsey, Dick Butler, Denis Murphy and Tom Quinn. They set to work immediately and launched their 'Blueprint for Change and Success for Dublin Hurling' in November 2001.

The introduction to the document made it clear what needed to be done.

'There must be an acceptance that the manner in which hurling in Dublin has been administered over the last 40 years has not been acceptable. This is clearly reflected by the lack of success and the decline in standards of hurling during this period. 1938 saw the last time that Dublin lifted the Liam MacCarthy Cup and 1961 was the last year Dublin reached a senior All-Ireland final. Since then, Dublin senior footballers have won six All-Ireland titles and 17 Leinster titles.

'The Dublin senior hurlers, during the same period, have not won a single provincial or national title.

'In order to improve standards and to achieve success, it is imperative that all aspects of administrations relating to the game are closely examined. Perhaps the greatest challenge facing us all is to change the mindset of those who are involved at all organisational levels. This mindset represents a shared way of thinking, and is reflected in the accepted behaviours and attitudes towards hurling in Dublin.

'In a mature association, such as the GAA, a shared mindset can be a liability, and its intensity may hinder its ability to change. Since members come to accept, adopt and associate with this mindset, the changing process requires that those who are in charge accept that change must happen, and must happen now. Charles Darwin once shrewdly observed that

It is not the strongest of the species that survives, nor the most intelligent, but those most responsive to change

'A truly empowered committee is one that acts out of commitment, out of purpose and without the traditional boundaries and narrow mindsets of previous administrators. In order for us to succeed, we must ensure that any recommendations put forward in this report, if accepted by the clubs, must be carried out within the appointed timeframe.'

The Report then went on to outline five key proposals.

1. Appoint a Director of Hurling
2. Devise new divisional and playing structures
3. Develop a highly skilled coaching programme
4. Provide top class facilities including a dedicated Hurling Centre incorporating an Academy of Excellence.
5. Introduce a dedicated hurling culture to project a dynamic image of Dublin Hurling

The report was well received by the Dublin County Board and the clubs. I must say that a lot of the proposals were delivered on, and of course there is still some work to be done.

Diarmuid Healy, former All-Ireland winning manager of Offaly, as well as managing his own county Kilkenny, was appointed Director of Hurling. He visited schools and clubs and worked very closely with the county board, games promotion officers, and county team managers. He was highly respected by all and his advice was valued and appreciated. I recall him telling one club that the grass height for a football game will not do for a hurling game. That was a surprise for some club officers.

I also recall him telling one senior manager that his plan for a training session was too fitness-oriented and there was not enough emphasis on skill and tactics. Nobody could question his knowledge of what was needed to produce successful top class hurlers and I believe he played a big part in laying the foundation for some of the successes of the following years.

Proposal 3 was about developing a highly skilled coaching programme. The Dublin County Board again made great progress in this area. John Costello, Kevin O'Shaughnessy and Ger O'Connor drove this and some excellent GPOs were appointed. All the development teams got excellent coaches, as did the coaches of the combined colleges teams.

It paid dividends.

We have had much more success at all levels in the past 21 years and well done to all concerned. The only disappointment that I have is that we won so few All-Ireland titles. Of course, that isn't the only benchmark of success.

The number of young people now playing hurling is growing by the year.

Damien Murphy, Dublin's juvenile secretary, reported recently that there was a 58% increase in the numbers involved in 'Go Games'. In the 13-16 age grade there was an increase in the number of teams participating, with football teams up 32% from 225 to 297, and hurling teams up 55% from 138 to 214. That is very satisfying.

Proposal 5 looked for a dedicated hurling culture to project a dynamic image of Dublin Hurling. As a result of the report, The Friends of Dublin Hurling was set up.

Michael O'Grady, Humphrey Kelleher, Tom O'Donnell, Peadar Mac Canna, Eugene Davey, Des O'Brien, Jim Browne, Michael Kilbride, Tom Quinn, Shay Boland and myself were there at the start, and we have now been joined by Ciarán Mac Annraoi, Eddie Glackin, Tony Evans, Máire Uí Scolaí, Alan Costello and Maeve Freeman.

I was very honoured to be asked join this committee as patron and we continue to promote Dublin hurling in various ways.

We run buses to away games. We hold Golf Classics every year.

We hold an Annual Celebration where we honour schools, clubs and players. Our average crowd for these nights is about 300 and we usually meet in The Red Cow Moran Hotel.

We support schools when they reach finals.

We honour a 'great' from the past with The Lar Foley Hall of Fame Award. Much to my surprise, I got the award in 2009. I had no idea I was getting it but when I saw my wife Gretta and my family coming into the room, I was totally perplexed and I felt I was losing it. However, I felt very honoured to receive it and join such distinguished company.

◄ ◄ ◆ ▷ ►

LAR FOLEY HALL OF FAME AWARD

2007 Jimmy Boggan	**2012** Tom Rock	**2017** Dick Fields
2008 Seán Óg Ó Ceallacháin	**2013** Con Ryan	**2018** Tom O'Donnell
2009 Jimmy Gray	**2014** Peadar Mac Canna	**2019** Jerry Grogan
2010 Fintan Walsh	**2015** Norman Allen	
2011 Con Clarke	**2016** Damien Byrne	

OVER THE PAST 16 years we have raised over €160,000 in support of Dublin hurling. This money has been principally raised in two main ways: FODH membership @ €20.00 per annum (our main source of funding) and our annual Golf Classic.

We maintain the FODH website (www.fodh.ie), and Facebook and Twitter accounts. At present we have approximately 500 members. Each month we hold a members' draw for match tickets, books and bus trips.

As I already said, I am delighted to be part of this group and I believe we have done a lot to promote a dynamic hurling culture in Dublin.

MY GREATEST TEAMS?

It's an impossible task really, especially when you can go back over 70 years. However, I have settled on the following for my best 15... for club, county, province and country.

NA FIANNA

Declan Feeney

Dermot McNulty   Pat Feeney   Michael O'Neill

Stephen Hegarty   Enda Gormley   Joe Casey

Joe Brennan   Mick Hayes

Donal Burke   Vinnie Bell   AJ Murphy

Johnny Keegan   Mick Kennedy   Seán Curry

DUBLIN

Kevin Mathews

Des Ferguson   Tomas Brady   John Finnegan

Joey Boland   Norman Allen   Liam Martin

Des Foley   Johnny McCaffrey

Achill Boothman   Conal Keaney   Donal Burke

Mick Birmingham   Kevin Flynn   Jack Finan

LEINSTER

Noel Skehan

Fan Larkin   Eugene Coughlan   Tom Neville

John Taylor   Norman Allen   Brian Whelahan

Des Foley   Ned Wheeler

Achill Boothman   Henry Shefflin   Conal Keaney

Oliver McGrath   Kieran Purcell   Eddie Keher

IRELAND

Noel Skehan

Fan Larkin   Eugene Coughlan   John Horgan

Tom Cashman   Norman Allen   Brian Whelahan

Des Foley   Joe Salmon

Achill Boothman   Conal Keaney   Jimmy Doyle

Christy Ring   Henry Shefflin   Eddie Keher

The Friends of Dublin Hurling honour Jimmy with the Lar Foley Hall of Fame Award (above) and one of the great thrills of Jimmy's life was getting to present the Leinster Championship trophy to Dublin captain Johnny McCaffrey after the historic victory in 2013.

« **EPILOGUE** »

THERE WAS ALWAYS music in our house, and down in Longford as well. My father loved Irish music. There was a chap in the Sugar Company and he was a member of the Bohemians, and he asked me to join them.

I thought he meant the Bohemians Football Club but, no, it was The Bohemian Musical Society. So I went down to the Montello Room in Jury's Hotel one Tuesday night to check it out. They played a lot of old Victorian ballads. I didn't fancy that.

I didn't go back for a while.

They were losing members, so my friend said to me, 'You have to join the Bohs… we all must get 10 new members to sign up!'

So, I eventually signed up. I went every Tuesday night and I began to enjoy it. The newer members introduced various different types of music. We all took turns at chairing the weekly sessions.

Each member could bring three guests and they could play three pieces, and members could play two pieces. I was the chairman one night and I decided to introduce some Irish music. I got Seán Potts, Mark Kelly and Paddy Glackin to come along. Seán's father was founder of *The Chieftains*. Paddy Glackin was a brilliant fiddle player. Mark Kelly is a guitar player with Altan who is married to my niece Frieda. They actually cancelled a night in Belfast to oblige me.

They played three pieces and the members loved it. From that night onwards, music became more mixed. I still go, and really enjoy it. My favourite music is Glenn Miller, but I enjoy opera and real traditional Irish music, especially fiddle playing. My favourite opera is *The Bohemian Girl*.

I HAD TAPES of *The Dubliners* in my car and I enjoyed listening to them as I travelled on business or to games. I knew Luke Kelly well, as he was a great friend of Jim King's. Both of them were members of O'Connell Boys. Luke was a lovely guy, but a little bit brash. We were in Mooney's Bar one night, across from the Gate Theatre, and Luke obviously said something wrong and the barman ordered Luke out... but with no great success.

Luke had a great voice for ballads and *Scorn Not His Simplicity* is a classic. We all loved *The Dubliners*. They were too fond of the drink, unfortunately. After a gig they would head to a pub for another session. One of the many stories told of them tells of the only non-drinker in the group, John Sheehan, giving the barman a fiver to close promptly at closing time as John had to go to work the following morning.

It rarely succeeded, as Luke or Ronnie Drew would give the barman a tenner to stay open. John and Heffo were pupils in Joeys, in Fairview. Colm O'Brien, John's pianist, was a brilliant performer. Most of those musicians started off with the tin whistle or the mouth organ and gradually progressed to be top class musicians.

ONE OF OUR neighbours in Longford, Matt Reilly was blind and he was a great fiddle player. He moved to St Joseph's in Drumcondra. He would come down to our house a few times every week and would play when the humour was on him. My mother decided that I should learn to play the fiddle.

So, she bought me a little fiddle and I was sent down to Mr Nolan in Clonliffe Road for lessons. I was doing okay, but when I started playing hurling and football in the primary school I lost interest in the fiddle. Matt, even though he was blind, would say to me, 'You are not holding the fiddle right!' He was a great man.

Matt went to Canada when he was 18 years of age and the job he got was herding sheep. He would light a fire at night to get a bit of heat, and the smoke from the fire eventually blinded him.

KEVIN HEFFERNAN INTRODUCED me to golf. One day, Lorcan Redmond invited me for a game of golf in his club, The Island. I couldn't hit the ball out of my way at the start, but it grew on me and eventually I joined the club for £140. I played there for about two years. Heffo said to me one day that I should be in Clontarf because a lot of GAA guys were members there. So, I joined Clontarf Golf Club for £120. I must say I really enjoyed the golf and the outings. I was blessed in the Sugar Company that I had about nine people in my department, when three would have sufficed. I could get away fairly often, and I played in lots of outings. I have the height of respect for Padraig Harrington and everything he has accomplished. His father was a great footballer; he played right half-back for the Garda team, and I was playing left half-forward for Na Fianna. I've also supported Paul McGinley.

Paul's father Mick came from Donegal and he was a member of Na Fianna. His first job was with Ciste na Banban pools. I played with Seán Clohosey, the man who got the last-minute goal in the 1960 Leinster final. He often said to me that he felt really sorry for Dublin that day, because a Dublin win would have meant so much to the game in Dublin.

I still enjoy playing twice a week in Clontarf, especially if I am in the company of Annmarie and my grandson Dara. My regular partners out on the course are Joe Rowley, Johnny Browne, Johnny Behan and sometimes John Costello. John hits the ball a mile, but not always straight. We all miss our very dear friend, the late Norman Allen, who also was such great company over 18 holes.

I SUPPORTED LIVERPOOL all my life.

The Scousers are great people and I enjoyed every day living among them. I had been working in London and hoping to get back to Dublin. My boss Michael Killeen said that he would take me out of London, but was sending me to Liverpool as the manager.

Liverpool had a poor reputation as a city then… rough and dirty.

The people made up for it… they were wonderful. They are half-Celts – Irish, Welsh and Scottish. I met a priest there by the name of Fr Speight. He was a wonderful character and a bit of a rebel. After ordination he went into the army as chaplain. He was on to the beaches of Normandy on D-Day. Some of his stories would make the hair stand on your head. One story was about when they went ashore, the chaplains came after the front line soldiers. One of the soldiers was injured and lying on the ground, and Fr Speight was also lying on the ground a few feet away.

He handed the host to a soldier nearest the wounded man, who gave it to dying soldier. Archbishop Heneghan heard about it and reprimanded him.

Nowadays, that's happening in all churches and lay people are giving the host to their fellow worshippers. So the good priest fell foul of Archbishop Heneghan. He was moved from parish to parish. He didn't have a drink problem, but he *liked* his drink. He got tired of parish life and became chaplain at Walton Gaol.

He was friendly with some board members of Liverpool and Everton football clubs. He would go to the home games every Saturday and I would often be his guest. John Moores was the boss of Littlewoods and he was on both boards. When I came back from holidays one year, I asked Fr Speight where we were going on Saturday?

'We are never going to Liverpool again!' he announced.

I was shocked, and asked why? He said John Smith, the chairman, had abused him. I was more than surprised because John was a very nice man. I asked Fr Speight to tell me more. He said he went into the boardroom after the game for drinks and John Smith stood up on a chair and said, 'Here's the papist!'

I am convinced to this day that John was only joking.

But that was the end of our trips to Anfield. We use to go to this small pub called The Harrington. Football was the normal topic of conversation and Fr Speight would usually be in the middle of some hot argument. I was talking to the barman one day about Fr Speight. He said that he had great time for the man. He said he renewed his faith in religion. He found him very natural and easy to talk to.

As a result he didn't convert but, he went to church every weekend.

I FOUND MYSELF in Windsor Park in November 1993 for the famous World Cup qualifier between Ireland and Northern Ireland for the 1994 World Cup finals. Through business, I had a few friends from Belfast who supported Northern Ireland.

I was in the Linfield soccer club boardroom before the game and I got a nice welcome. I felt a bit intimidated at the game itself as I had some staunch

Northern Ireland supporters all around me. Alan McLoughlin got the crucial equaliser late in the second-half and I am glad he didn't hear some of the abuse that we heard in the stand. All was quiet after the game and the only place we could get a bit of food was in a pub on the Shankill Road.

I felt very safe as I was with my friends who were wonderful hosts.

Sport has been good to me all my life and I still enjoy attending as many games as possible. I don't know how I would pass away my time if I hadn't an interest in sport.

Hurling, gaelic football... every single sport.

Jimmy and Gretta celebrate their 55th wedding anniversary with their family in 2014 and (below) Jimmy enjoys quality time with his grandchildren.

MORE
GREAT
SPORTS BOOKS
FROM
HEROBOOKS

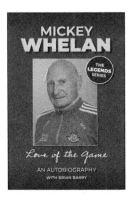

LOVE OF THE GAME
Mickey Whelan: An Autobiography

MICKEY WHELAN IS one of Ireland's greatest coaching masters. He is a father figure for all of those who sought sporting excellence in this country over the last 50 years. He was the inspirational mind behind the creation of Kevin Heffernan's amazing Dublin team of the 70s, which won three All-Ireland titles and changed the face of Gaelic football forever. A former All-Ireland winner with Dublin in 1963, Whelan also managed Dublin himself in the 90s.

A fitter by profession, the Clanna Gael and St Vincent's man interrupted his own career and emigrated to the United States with his family in 1969. He returned home with a Masters in Sports Science. He has worked on the academic staff of DIT Bolton St and DCU.

Whelan was at Pat Gilroy's side as Dublin reclaimed the All-Ireland title in 2011 – thereby spring-boarding the creation of the greatest football team in GAA history.

Author: Brian Barry
Hardback: €25.00
Paperback: €20.00
Ebook: €9.99
ISBN: 9781910827352

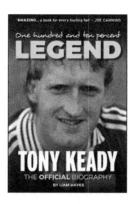

One Hundred and Ten Percent Legend
Tony Keady: The Official Biography

WHEN TONY KEADY died suddenly in August of 2017, at just 53 years of age, a whole county mourned and the rest of the country stopped in its tracks to say goodbye to a legend of the game of hurling.

In 1988, after leading Galway to a second All-Ireland title in succession, he was crowned the greatest hurler in Ireland. He was 25 years of age and there was nobody like him, nobody to touch him in the maroon No.6 shirt. But, four years later, and still not 30, after being wrongly banned for 12 months by the GAA, he was also discarded by his own county and refused a maroon jersey the very last time he walked out onto Croke Park behind the Galway team.

A few months before his death, Tony Keady visited Liam Hayes and told him he wished to tell his own story. He felt it was time, but tragically time was not on Tony's side. Tony's wife Margaret and his daughter Shannon and his three boys Anthony, Harry and Jake, decided to finish telling the story of a father and a hurler who always asked those around him for '110%'.

Author: Liam Hayes
Hardback: €25.00
Paperback: €20.00
Ebook: €9.99
ISBN: 9781910827048

Buy on **Amazon**
(and paperback available in all good bookstores)

'A Game that Smiles'
Richie Bennis: An Autobiography

RICHIE BENNIS IS one of the true legends remaining in the game of hurling. A towering figure in Limerick GAA, he played a central role as the county won the All-Ireland title in 1973 and then he strived as hard as anyone to see the Liam MacCarthy Cup return to the Treaty County.

It was a wait of 45 years – during which time Bennis worked at grassroots hurling in the famed Patrickswell club, where he hurled into his 40s and won 10 county titles. He also led Limerick as team manager to the 2007 All-Ireland final where they lost to Kilkenny.

In 2018, Limerick were crowned All-Ireland champions.

For Richie Bennis, a long agonising wait ended. His story is one of triumph, and heartache and personal tragedy, and a courage that was never dimmed.

Authors: Richie Bennis with Ciarán Kennedy
Hardback: €25.00
Paperback: €20.00
Ebook: €9.99
ISBN: 9781910827093

Buy on **Amazon**
(and paperback available in all good bookstores)

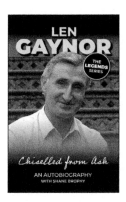

Chiselled from Ash
Len Gaynor: An Autobiography

CHISELLED FROM ASH is a story of love and honour.

It's the story of Len Gaynor's great love for the game of hurling, and how he has honoured the great game his whole life.

Len Gaynor won it all with Tipperary, finishing his career with three All-Ireland hurling titles, four Munster titles and two National League titles in the 1960s and 70s. But the flamboyant wing back also wanted to give back at the end of his career.

The Kilruane MacDonaghs clubman – and winner of three county titles – quickly proved himself to be one of the smartest and most ambitious coaches in the game. At club level he strived to teach and help the next generation, and led his own Kilruane and neighbouring clubs to success – and at county level through the 1990s Len Gaynor managed Tipperary and Clare on the biggest stages in the game.

Authors: Len Gaynor with Shane Brophy

Hardback: €25.00

Paperback: €20.00

Ebook: €9.99

ISBN: 9781910827208

Buy on **Amazon**
(and paperback available in all good bookstores)

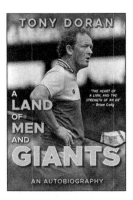

A Land of Men and Giants
The Tony Doran Autobiography

WEXFORD'S ALL-IRELAND winning hero Tony Doran was a giant in the game of hurling through the 1960s, 70s and 80s, at a time when full-forwards were ordered to plunder goals. In his 19 years and 187 appearances as a Wexford hurler, Tony Doran successfully went for goal 131 times. But Doran also played against giants from Kilkenny, Tipperary and Cork, and so many other counties, at a time when the game of hurling tested the wits and the courage of every man on the field.

Some of these men became giants.

A Land of Men and Giants is the story told by Tony Doran of a life spent living and competing against legendary men and true giants of the game.

A Land of Men and Giants: The Autobiography of Tony Doran is edited by award-winning writer and author Liam Hayes.

Authors: Tony Doran with Liam Hayes
Hardback: €25.00
Paperback: €20.00
Ebook: €9.99
ISBN: 9781910827031

Buy on **Amazon**
(and paperback available in all good bookstores)

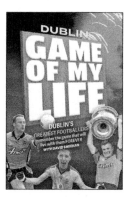

DUBLIN
GAME OF MY LIFE

25 OF THE GREATEST DUBLIN footballers over the last 60 years remember the one game in their careers that defined their sporting lives.

Including: Jim Crowley, Bernard Brogan Snr, Paddy Cullen, Tommy Drumm, Tommy Conroy, Gerry Hargan, Johnny Magee, Paddy Christie, Paul Curran, Vinnie Murphy, Kevin Nolan, Charlie Redmond, Paul Griffin, Ray Cosgrove, John O'Leary, Barney Rock, Kieran Duff, Jack Sheedy, Alan Larkin, Robbie Kelleher, Shane Ryan, Ger Brennan, Tommy Carr, Ciarán Whelan, Collie Moran and Alan Brogan

A game that will live with each person forever.

Author: David Sheehan
Hardback: €25.00
Paperback: €20.00
Ebook: €9.99
ISBN: 9781910827383

Buy on **Amazon**
(and paperback available in all good bookstores)

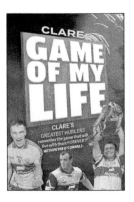

CLARE
GAME OF MY LIFE

30 OF THE GREATEST CLARE hurlers over the last 60 years remember the one game in their careers that defined their sporting lives.

Including: Naoise Jordan, Jackie O'Gorman, Seamus Durack, Sean O'Hehir, Colm Honan, Sean Stack, Tommy Keane, Tommy Guilfoyle, David Forde, Ollie Baker, Stephen McNamara, Frank Lohan, Fergie Tuohy, Gerry McInerney, Fergal Hegarty, Ger Loughnane, Niall Gilligan, Gerry Quinn, Anthony Daly, Brian O'Connell, Fergal Lynch, Cian Dillon, Podge Collins, Brendan Bugler, Pat O'Connor, Colin Ryan, Patrick Donnellan, Conor Ryan, John Conlon and Tony Kelly

A game that will live with each person forever.

Author: Peter O'Connell
Hardback: €25.00
Paperback: €20.00
Ebook: €9.99
ISBN: 9781910827376

Buy on **Amazon**
(and paperback available in all good bookstores)

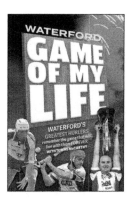

WATERFORD
GAME OF MY LIFE

25 OF THE GREATEST WATERFORD hurlers over the last 60 years remember the one game in their careers that defined their sporting lives.

Including: Tom Cunningham, Martin Óg Morrissey, Michael O'Connor, Larry Guinan, Jim Greene, Brian Greene, Patricia Jackman, Mossie Walsh, John Galvin, Shane Ahearne, Stephen Frampton, Fergal Hartley, Sean Cullinane, Brian Flannery, Eoin Murphy, John Mullane, Beth Carton , Paul Flynn , Dan Shanahan and Maurice Shanahan

A game that will live with each person forever.

Author: Tómas McCarthy
Hardback: €25.00
Paperback: €20.00
Ebook: €9.99
ISBN: 9781910827406

Buy on **Amazon**
(and paperback available in all good bookstores)

TIPPERARY
GAME OF MY LIFE

THE GREATEST TIPPERARY hurlers over the last 50 years remember the one game in blue and gold that defined their lives...

Including: Jimmy Finn, Theo English, Tony Wall, Tadhg O'Connor, Dinny Ryan, Babs Keating, John Sheedy, Ken Hogan, Colm Bonnar, Cormac Bonnar, Declan Carr, Michael Cleary, Pat Fox, Conal Bonnar, Declan Ryan, Michael Ryan, Joe Hayes, Eamonn Corcoran, Tommy Dunne, Shane McGrath, James Woodlock, Brendan Cummins, Eoin Kelly, Michael Cahill, Brendan Maher, James Barry, Seamus Callinan and more...

A game that will live with each person forever.

Author: Stephen Gleeson
Hardback: €25.00
Paperback: €20.00
Ebook: €9.99
ISBN: 9781910827185

Buy on **Amazon**
(and paperback available in all good bookstores)

GALWAY
GAME OF MY LIFE

TWENTY-FIVE OF GALWAY'S greatest hurlers remember the one game that will live with them forever...

Including: Jimmy Hegarty, Ned Dervan, Andy Fenton, Iggy Clarke, Sean Silke, Joe Connolly, PJ Molloy, Noel Lane, John Connolly, Mike Conneely, Anthony Cunningham, Pete Finnerty, Eanna Ryan, Gerry McInerney, John Commins, Michael Coleman, Micheál Donoghue, Padraig Kelly, Kevin Broderick, Ger Farragher, David Collins, Ollie Canning, Alan Kerins, Fergal Moore and Gearoid McInerney.

A game that will live with each person forever.

Author: Ollie Turner
Hardback: €25.00
Paperback: €20.00
Ebook: €9.99
ISBN: 9781910827284

Buy on **Amazon**
(and paperback available in all good bookstores)

Printed in Great Britain
by Amazon

79640107R00123